Letting Go
One Step At a Time

Beyond Controloholism

Maynard Dalderis
and
Leanne Dalderis

Text Design and Layout
Kelly Hewkin, IntuitiveGraphicDesign.com

Letting Go One Step At A Time: Beyond Controloholism
ISBN 978-0-921154-21-1

Maynard Dalderis and Leanne Dalderis

Publisher
Guideline Productions Inc.
Calgary, Alberta, Canada
e| dalderis@vitagenics.ca
w| www.livingwithguidance.ca

Beyond Controloholism Are All Life's Gifts, Waiting To Be Given

Beyond our tears there is laughter.

Beyond our despair there is hope.

Beyond our loneliness we find each other.

Beyond our fears there is release.

Beyond our controls there is freedom.

Beyond everything there is Love.

*Let us walk together beyond all these things
to receive the gift of Life.*

In Deep Gratitude We Acknowledge...

The Guidance we refer to as our "Sponsor" that in a manner, not unlike that of A Course In Miracles, literally dictated most of this manuscript.

All the 12 step programs that have already proven that our addictions can be overcome; with special thanks to the AA pioneers who courageously paved the way in an uncharted territory – successfully.

Stephen R. Alger for sponsoring the 1ˢᵗ printing of this book.

Sharma Hodgson of Synchronicity Magazine for the cover graphics.

Kelly Hewkin for text design and layout.

Gary Craig's Emotional Freedom Technique, which we find to be a marvellous catalyst to speed up this process.

Participants of our Wednesday night open group that cradled many of these ideas over 14 years of meetings.

All our fellow controloholics; while pointing out your controls, we received an opportunity to see our own.

We further thank our Guidance, who when asked what lies beyond controloholism, said that we would be aware of the true spiritual Gifts of God such as Peace, Unconditional Love, Joy, Happiness, Grace, Innocence, Beauty, Trust, Support... patiently waiting for us, the moment we were willing to release "our" solution, "our" controls.

The Guidance then dictated another book entitled, **The Gift Book** *(110 Gifts in all) as a follow-up to* **Letting Go One Step At A Time, Beyond Controloholism***.*

Mostly, thanks to a Loving God, to make this healing message possible.

Introduction

This book is a gift. It is a gift to us and we hope you will see its gift to you. Our sponsor gave us the gift of his caring, each time we ran into difficulty understanding and following the twelve steps of this Program. Each time we were confused and in conflict, he would bring us back to the wisdom of the Twelve Step Program and show how each step worked towards releasing our difficulties and healing our lives. He said if we wanted another way out of our life of misery, fear and struggle, the program was for us. With a willingness to follow the steps, the program would both change and bring Peace into our lives.

After each discussion, our sponsor would have us write what he had shared about the program. We acknowledge our sponsor for the writings that are contained in this book, and we acknowledge our Higher Power for the gift of our sponsor, and for the gift of His guidance. We have included our own sharing whenever we felt called upon to share the lessons and learnings that have touched us.

We owe so much to the gift of the A.A. Twelve Step Program. It is a Program that works and continues to work for so many of us — from the hopeless alcoholic and addict to the hopeless controloholic in all of us. It is a program of the heart, for ultimately that is all any of us can share — the gift of our hearts.

We've included the teachings of our sponsor exactly as they were given to us. Our own sharing is included wherever we felt that our stories might assist fellow controloholics in some way.

This is not a book of methods. This is not a book of how-tos. This is not a book of fixing or of explanations. It is a book of hope. It is a book of release and solutions. It is a book of sharing and gratitude. And with the guidance of our Higher Power, it is a book that shows another way. It is a book for anyone who is willing to recover from and go beyond a life run by controls. And it is a book for those who wish to discover the incredible gifts that the promise of another way holds for us.

A Road to Recovery

Beyond Controloholism is neither meant as a replacement for any twelve step group, nor is it an umbrella for all twelve step groups. It is simply a program "to practice these principles in *all* our affairs". It is a program that includes our very specific addictions and also the very broad base of controls that underlies all addictions.

Specific identification of our addictions is most necessary for their release. Specific programs, then, are heartily encouraged. We need to look specifically at what "solutions" we have used to run our lives with.

There will also come a point where we need to apply this program in all areas of our lives. This is the aim of *Beyond Controloholism*. We will need to look at all areas we have attempted to control or manage.

Beyond Controloholism does not replace anything; it may, in fact, be used as a beginning point where those looking at their controls are directed to more specific programs for addictions that have greatly controlled their lives.

Recovery goes both ways — from a specific addiction to all areas of our lives, and again from all areas to very specific addictions that we each must acknowledge and release.

The bottom line is — the program works. We practice these principles in all areas of our lives. It is to this end or beginning that *Beyond Controloholism* offers its insights and most importantly, its sharing.

No, *Beyond Controloholism* isn't a replacement, nor an umbrella — it is a two way street. It is a street that goes to specific recovery, and it is a street that brings recovery to all parts of our lives.

With this Twelve Step Program, we are on the road to recovery.

We only ask that our Higher Power maintains the Program in our lives and gives us the strength to share this program with anyone who desires another way of living rather than a life based on self-will and destruction.

Letting Go of Trying to Control Life

We do not give up our controls in order to be at the mercy of everyone and everything; we give up our controls in order to feel the safety of loving Guidance.

We do not give up our controls in order to lose all sense of who we are; we give up our controls to finally find who we are and our tremendous connection with all those in our lives.

We do not give up our controls in order to lose; we give up our controls in order to gain a sense of freedom and release.

We do not give up our controls in order to mindlessly drift about; we give up our controls in order to be at the center of all that unfolds through and around us.

We do not give up our controls in order to lose our very survival; we give up our controls so that we may be given Life - we may thrive.

We do not give up our controls so that nothing gets done or accomplished; we give up our controls so that finally, what is appropriate for all healing may be accomplished.

We do not give up our controls in order to become lost; we give up our controls in order to find our connection with All Life and All Being.

We do not give up our controls in order to be controlled; we give up our controls so that a solution may be seen beyond our "controloholism".

We do not give up our controls in order to be without direction; we give up our controls in order to finally find the direction of a loving God.

Ultimately, we do not give up our controls to God to live with second best; we give up our controls to God so the very best may occur.

Table of Contents

Starting From Where We Are

"I always thought that I had to know everything. I never let myself be a beginner."

We give ourselves the freedom to begin; we give ourselves the freedom to be a beginner.

We are newcomers to the Truth each moment.

Our Goal

Our goal is not to get others to see — it is for us to see.

Our goal is not to be right — it is to give up this judgment in order to be happy.

Our goal is not to decide what should be done — our goal is to decide: "Thy Will be done."

Our goal is not to force an issue — our goal is to let go of all outcomes of any issues.

Our goal is not of correction — it is of forgiveness.

Our goal is not to justify — our goal is admittance so our Higher Power can correct mistaken perceptions.

Our goal is not to secure our safety — it is to give our very safe-keeping to our Higher Power.

Our goal is not to avenge anything — it is to see Peace.

Our goal is not to take a side — our goal is to join with others in seeing Innocence.

Our goal is not to condemn — it is to accept.

Our goal is not to be in charge — our goal is to be gently guided.

Our goal is not to know — our goal is to be given knowing.

Our goal is not to take over — it is to let go.

Our Experience

People would come to us for consultation. Time and time again we saw that their problems stemmed from what they were trying to control. They came to us not wanting to give up control or management — they came so we could tell them how to make their controls work better.

At first, it was very frustrating to relate to these people without the Program. We could see how the Twelve Step Program worked in our lives, keeping us straight and sober. We saw the sanity and healing that the Program brought to us and yet people coming to us were not always alcoholics or drug users. They did not overwork or overeat. They weren't addicted to gambling or shopping. Yet, all their symptoms were the same as those of us in the A.A. Program. They, too, seemed to be addicted just as we were addicted. How did the Program relate to them?

Then we saw the connection. We were all addicted to control. Whether we abused substances or people, we were all addicted, in one form or another, to control. We were all "controloholics". The same Program that worked for us, we found, could work on any addiction. And what greater addiction do we all share than controloholism?

So, we began to use the same Twelve Step Program that has been so successful with alcoholics and drug users, with anyone who came with a problem. We told them about the only way that has worked for us and other addicts of control. We had to admit that our attempts at controlling situations was the problem. At first they were angry and disappointed when we told them that perhaps their very controls were the problem. They didn't want to hear this. They wanted the magic control or treatment that was going to work. They wanted a band-aid to cover up the pain so they didn't have to look at their own attempts to control in the situation. "Give me anything but don't ask me to give up control!"

We told them that once we admitted our addiction to control, we became willing to ask a Power greater than ourselves to restore us to Sanity. This, at first, was not popular either, for God, in most of these people's lives, was not something they could rely on. If anything, they had avoided reference to the whole idea of God.

That's when we put them in touch with the idea of Completeness or Wholeness within us. Instead of the Holy Spirit, it became the Spirit of Wholeness. We talked about other names for the Higher Power such as: Love, Trust, Support, Integrity, Knowing. We asked them to consider asking for Knowing in a situation, for a solution, rather than for methods in how to control the situation.

We told them that we had found that controlling only chokes off answers or solutions, while considering this higher aspect of Support and Integrity opens us to all the opportunities for answers, for another way. We found it is so important to have that concept or feeling of a Higher Power, of a Higher Self, because

*it isn't that we give up on control, we give up control
to that part of ourselves that is in touch with all the
answers; the part that is all-knowing. It sounded
kind of hokey to those wishing to maintain control
but there was a question we always asked those in
difficulty when they wanted to hold onto their controls
— "How is it working so far?"*

*We found that without the knowledge of a Higher
Power, giving up controls meant nothing to anyone. It
only meant there was no control at all, for where was
it going to come from, if they were not controlling?
More and more, we find there is a spiritual thirst to
get in touch with a Power greater than ourselves that
can restore order and sanity in our lives. Those who
have come to see us have had such an aversion to
spirituality, to a Power greater than themselves. Their
beliefs in God have been warped, abused, misused
and fraught with guilt. They have not wanted to turn
their controls over to such a being — it has seemed
far safer to do it on their own.*

Maynard and Leanne

Who Is A Controloholic?

We found *we* were controloholic, when we sought to control those around us with *our* solutions. We found we were controloholic, when these solutions became more important than anything or anyone around us. We found we became controloholics, when *our* will came first, when our desperations were placed above all else.

We find we continue to be controloholics, whenever we choose "my way not Thy Way be done." We find we are still controloholics, when *our* solutions for happiness are placed above the solution our *Higher Power* would give us. We find we are controloholic, when we seek to control, and we seek to control in almost every aspect of our lives.

We are controloholic, when we wish to manage the outcome of a situation.

Who is a controloholic? — We are, when we seek to manage or control our lives.

But the moment we decide, "I no longer wish to be controlled by controls," then, in that moment, do we go beyond our addiction. When we give our lives to our Higher Power, then in that moment is our addiction released. When we decide to ask for another way beyond our controls, do we go beyond controloholism.

What Is Controloholism?

Controloholism is simply our addiction to *our* solutions that we have sought to control our lives with. Controloholism is a desperate attempt to manage the world as *we* think it should be. It is a reliance on *our* solutions, rather than seeking *God's* solution.

Controloholism is a life run on self-will. It is a life run on a strong desire to be right about our solutions, about what we think should bring us happiness. There is no area of our lives that this affliction does not touch. Trying to control is a state of *dis-ease*, for we are no longer at *Ease* with our Higher Power.

Controloholism does not care for consequences; it only cares to be in control at all costs. We, who choose to control, have felt the loneliness and separation of this dis-ease. Controloholism is simply a desire to control *our* way.

Here we wish to go beyond controloholism, because this dis-ease has made our lives separate and painful. We wish to go beyond the fear that controloholism brings. We wish to go beyond the anguish and desperation that our controloholism always brings. We wish to go *beyond* controloholism.

Are You A Controloholic?

These questions have been inspired from the 20 questions used by alcoholics to discover their drinking problems. We find them very useful to remind us that our controloholism is indeed a problem and affects every aspect of our lives. We invite you to answer the questions as honestly as possible. If you answer "yes" to 3 or more of these questions, then there is a strong possibility that you are a controloholic.

1. Have you ever tried to control something so much that you had to miss time from work? ☐ Y ☐ N

2. Is your insistence on being in control making your home life unhappy? ☐ Y ☐ N

3. Do you try to control because you feel insecure with other people? ☐ Y ☐ N

4. Are your attempts to control making those around you ill at ease and wishing to avoid you? ☐ Y ☐ N

5. Have you ever felt remorse after certain attempts to control someone or something? ☐ Y ☐ N

6. Has trying to control certain areas of your life ever brought you financial difficulty? ☐ Y ☐ N

7. Do you place yourself in risky and uncomfortable situations when you are trying to control certain things in your life? ☐ Y ☐ N

8. Does your intent to control ever make you careless of your family's feelings and welfare? ☐ Y ☐ N

9. Do your attempts to control make you feel tired and worn out? ☐ Y ☐ N

10. Do you try to control any situation in which you are fearful? In other words, does uncertainty make you want to control? [Y] [N]

11. Do you ever begin your day thinking of how you want it to go and how you could control it to go that way? [Y] [N]

12. Do you ever lose sleep from worrying about the things you have to control? [Y] [N]

13. Has your creativity and spontaneity decreased as a result of your trying to control? [Y] [N]

14. Have you ever been so uptight from your efforts to control that your job or business suffered? [Y] [N]

15. Do you have so many things you feel you need to control that you find it necessary to escape from time to time by either: drinking, taking drugs, overeating, seeking excitement, sleeping, reading, exercising, travelling... and so on? [Y] [N]

16. When you are bent on controlling, do you feel alone? [Y] [N]

17. Are you so intent on controlling at times that you forget what is important to family and friends? Is your tunnel of control blocking others' needs from your sight? [Y] [N]

18. Has your desire to control brought about any disease condition or feeling of dis-ease due to the tension created? [Y] [N]

19. Do you try to control in order to make yourself "good" enough? [Y] [N]

20. Have the things you wished to control ever been so consuming that counselling or hospitalization was necessary? [Y] [N]

Anyone who is disappointed by a "low" score, by scoring less than 10 yes's, I would heartily suggest that you ask your spouse, partner, parents, brothers, sisters, children, friends, or co-workers to answer these questions for you. I guarantee that your score will "improve" and you'll be able to count yourself amongst the "elite" fellowship of controloholics. Welcome home!

Question: *Isn't everyone then a controloholic? I can't think of anyone who is not.*

Answer: *You may be right. We just might be in the middle of an epidemic.*

                              — Maynard

For Good Measure

In case we have doubts about our controloholism, our sponsor has included some additional questions to help us make up our minds:

1. Do you find yourself serious most of the time so that having fun is difficult for you? <kbd>Y</kbd> <kbd>N</kbd>

2. Do you find yourself feeling insecure and lonely even in the company of others? <kbd>Y</kbd> <kbd>N</kbd>

3. Have you ever felt yourself living a life of quiet desperation? <kbd>Y</kbd> <kbd>N</kbd>

4. Do you often hide your true feelings? <kbd>Y</kbd> <kbd>N</kbd>

5. Do you **either** try to make everything "smooth" or try to disrupt and stir things up? <kbd>Y</kbd> <kbd>N</kbd>

6. Do you have long lists and reminders of what you would like to see accomplished and do you get upset if these aren't fulfilled? <kbd>Y</kbd> <kbd>N</kbd>

7. Do you ever find yourself needing explanations or having to explain nearly everything? <kbd>Y</kbd> <kbd>N</kbd>

8. Have you been engaged in judging others, yet fearful of being judged yourself? <kbd>Y</kbd> <kbd>N</kbd>

9. Do you become upset if events do not go as planned? <kbd>Y</kbd> <kbd>N</kbd>

10. Do you get caught up in either resenting or defending authority? <kbd>Y</kbd> <kbd>N</kbd>

11. Do you find yourself avoiding many activities because you cannot control the outcome? <kbd>Y</kbd> <kbd>N</kbd>

12. Do you either resist change, or do you seek change frequently in order to get away from unhappiness? ☐Y ☐N

13. Do you need other people to make you happy? ☐Y ☐N

14. Do you find yourself avoiding people, places and things that upset you? ☐Y ☐N

15. Do you ever find yourself worried about the future and/or resentful of the past? ☐Y ☐N

16. Do you sometimes feel the need to fix and manage other people's lives? ☐Y ☐N

17. Do other people's actions often upset you? ☐Y ☐N

18. Do you feel responsible for pleasing and making others happy? ☐Y ☐N

19. Do you frequently find yourself defending and looking for an excuse to cover your actions? ☐Y ☐N

20. Do you at times feel unfairly treated — a victim of circumstance? ☐Y ☐N

21. Have you found yourself trying to do the right thing and not knowing what it is? ☐Y ☐N

22. Do you go to great lengths to get your way? ☐Y ☐N

23. Do you fear what people may think of you? ☐Y ☐N

24. Do you feel others expect a lot of you that you cannot fulfill? ☐Y ☐N

25. Do you have difficulty letting people get close to you? ☐Y ☐N

Our aim here is not to discourage; our aim is to show what we may finally be free from. There are very few of us who do not seek to control at some time or another. These questions are not asked to make us feel guilty — they are asked in order to assist us in seeing what we may finally let go of. No, our focus is not to make each other feel bad with all the controls we may use — our focus is release. Our focus is to go beyond those things that have controlled and blocked our growth. The point is, we wish to make room in our lives — more room for Love, more room for Joy, more room for others, and more room for the Presence of a Higher Power.

The Twelve Steps

Beyond controloholism is not to keep our controls; it is to go beyond them. This is a program of discovery and recovery. In our admittance of controloholism, we discover a program that will lead us to recovery. The same steps that have so helped those with addictions will lead us beyond this addiction to go beyond our controls and what controls us. These are the steps we follow:

1. "We admitted that we were powerless over control in our lives — that we could neither control nor manage our own lives."

2. "We came to believe that a Power greater than ourselves could restore us to sanity."

3. "We made a decision to turn our will and our lives over to the care of God as we understood Him."

4. "We made a searching and fearless moral inventory of ourselves."

5. "We admitted to God, to ourselves, and to another human being the exact nature of our wrongs."

6. "We were entirely ready to have God remove all these defects of character."

7. "We humbly asked God to remove our shortcomings."

8. "We made a list of all persons we had harmed, and became willing to make amends to them all."

9. "We made direct amends to such people wherever possible, except when to do so would injure them or others."

10. We continued to take personal inventory and when we were wrong, promptly admitted it."

11. "We sought through prayer and meditation to improve our conscious contact with God, as we understood Him, praying only for the knowledge of His will for us and the power to carry that out."

12. "Having had a spiritual awakening as a result of these steps, we became willing to carry this message to other controloholics, and to practice these principles in all our affairs."

The Twelve Steps of Alcoholics Anonymous

1. We admitted that we were powerless over alcohol — that our lives had become unmanageable.

2. Came to believe that a Power greater than ourselves could restore us to sanity.

3. Made a decision to turn our will and our lives over to the care of God as we understood Him.

4. Made a searching and fearless moral inventory of ourselves.

5. Admitted to God, to ourselves, and to another human being the exact nature of our wrongs.

6. Were entirely ready to have God remove all these defects of character.

7. Humbly asked Him to remove our shortcomings.

8. Made a list of all persons we had harmed and became willing to make amends to them all.

9. Made direct amends to such people wherever possible, except when to do so would injure them or others.

10. Continued to take personal inventory and when we were wrong, promptly admitted it.

11. Sought through prayer and meditation to improve our conscious contact with God as we understood Him, praying only for the knowledge of His will for us and the power to carry that out.

12. Having had a spiritual awakening as a result of these steps, we became willing to carry this message to other alcoholics, and to practice these principles in all our affairs.

The Twelve Steps are reprinted with permission of Alcoholics Anonymous World Services Inc. Permission to reprint and adapt the Twelve Steps does not mean that A.A. is in any way affiliated with this publication. A.A. is a program of recovery from alcoholism. Use of the Twelve Steps in connection with programs and activities which are patterned after A.A. but which address other problems does not imply otherwise.

Admitting A Program Of Recovery

This Is A Simple Program

We saw how the alcoholic wished to control the world through his drinking. Drinking was seen as a way to control both himself and his relationship to his environment. The A.A. Big Book describes the source of the disease as "self-will run riot". This definition, we found, was also the underlying cause of the disease of controloholism. We tried to control with our self-will in many different ways — some of them obvious, some of them not. And when our controls did not work, we had addictions to maintain the sense of control. We drank, we took drugs, we ate, we slept, we read, we had countless relationships, we gambled, we shopped, we worked, we exercised, we were in abusive relationships, we travelled — all with the obsession of gaining some sense of order or control in our lives.

We sought control — and our lives were uncontrollable. We sought freedom from being controlled — and had never felt more imprisoned. We sought order — and found only chaos. For a while, we had a sense of control — but at such a cost. Always did we feel things were never fully in control and may soon be out of control.

We found that each time we wanted to control, each situation that we tried to control brought tension and disease. We found we could not control anything through our self-will. We found our lives were being controlled by the very controls we used. If we tried to control by working — working controlled us. If we tried to control by analyzing — then analyzing controlled all of our affairs. If we tried to control our relationships — then our relationships obsessed us. If we tried to control by eating — then eating overcame us. If we tried to control by having order — then order suffocated us. If we tried to control by arranging the universe — then our arrangements overwhelmed us. Whatever we sought to control brought us tension and disease. And like any addiction, the more we used control, the more it was needed. The more we sought to control, the more addicted we became; and the more addicted we became, the more we were afraid to let go of our controls.

We were trying so hard to control that we believed to let go would bring total chaos. We tried to control and our lives were out of control. Just as an alcoholic's drinking was out of control, we found that we, too, could not stop — our controls were out of control. We found that we had to rely on a Power greater than ourselves to stop our addiction and to bring order into our lives.

Sometimes our addictions were not dramatic. We were not always alcoholics, drug users, workaholics, gamblers, shopaholics; we did not have sexual perversions or necessarily come from these types of backgrounds. But, although we did not necessarily have these symptoms — we were addicted to control. We sought to control our lives and found our lives controlled. We were afraid, unhappy and in despair.

We did not always have observable addictions, but we found we were addicted just the same. We were addicted to our controls and the using of our solutions. Just as with the alcoholic, the problem in our lives was "self-will run riot". We found the same program that helped the alcoholic and the drug addict was applicable in our lives. It was the same problem with the same solution. We might or might not take drugs. We might or might not be abusive. We might or might not drink. It did not matter. The disease was controloholism — wanting to control in any way we could. The solution went beyond the using of our will, to our finding God's Will. And in this, whatever the symptoms of the addiction, we found we are all the same. We call ourselves *controloholics*.

Users

And, so, we found we were users. We were users of all sorts of controls. We were users of guilt, pain, unhappiness, niceness, anger, blame, worry, force, willpower, manipulation, charm, lies, sickness, pleasing, pushing, procrastination — anything that would control ourselves and those around us.

We found ourselves in the company of the more sensational addicts. We did not think our problem was as great as theirs, but we soon saw that unhappiness and desperation makes no distinction. Our lives too were unmanageable and out of control, whether we were addicts of drugs or addicts of manipulation. It was all the same. We were all controloholics. We were finally willing to give up our aversion to seeing ourselves like the drunk or the drug addict. As users we were abusers. We were willing to see, that no matter what was used, our addiction to control made us the same as any other addict.

And, if we were alcoholic, we found that alcohol was not our only symptom of addiction. If we used drugs or work or any other addiction, we found that these were not our only symptoms. We too had many other controls that we were addicted to using in our search to manage our lives. We too were users of anything that would control.

And, so, as users we come together, despite our symptoms, to let go of what has controlled us. We come together to let go of the controls that we have been using. We come together to let go of our self-will in order to have God's Will for us. We had used, and now we come to be of use. We ask God to manage our using and make us of use to each other.

We Began To See

We began to see how many things we wished to control each day. We wished to control the time we had. We wished to control with a certain plan that must take place. We wished to control another's appearance. We wished to control our partner in business. We wished to control what we ate, where we slept, how much money we made. We wished to control traffic, government. We wished to control our partners, children, parents, friends. We even wished to control our pets, our plants, our home. We began to see all the things that were caught up in our controls.

We began to see how controlled our lives were, for in trying to control we also were controlled — controlled by our own misery in trying to control. We began to see that we were powerless over stopping our controls; we were powerless over managing our lives. The more we sought control, the more we felt we did not have it and the more controlled our lives seemed to be.

We began to see that by ourselves our controls were too much for us. We began to see there was an order in our life, there was a plan, but that order or plan was not brought about by our controls.

We had tried to control everything, and now we were willing to consider giving up the controls of our self-will for the order of God's Will. We became willing to ask that God's Will replace the desperation of our controls. We began to see there was order to the universe by being willing to give up *our* order, *our* controls.

Giving Up To

At times, in our controloholic addiction, we came to the point where, control as we might, nothing seemed to work. We tried all our controls but the situation only worsened. At this point, we *gave up on* whatever it was or whoever it was we were trying to control. We had given up on many ideas, institutions, places, situations, relationships; and in our controloholic state, we continued to give up on what no longer appeared to work.

As controloholics we gave up on life, when life seemed no longer to be able to be controlled. We even gave up on some of our controls and continued to be in desperation.

We finally found that the only thing that worked was not giving up *on* but giving up *to* a Higher Power. We found that giving up *on* led to desperation and disappointment. We found that giving up *to* led to healing and to Peace. We gave up on, when *we* were in control or trying to be in control. We gave up *to,* when we realized our controls no longer worked and we wished the solution of our Higher Power. We realized that what we gave up *on* could not be healed. What we gave up *to* our Higher Power, including all our controls, could be released and seen another way. We found we had to give up *to* God everything that we had sought to control in order to have *His* solution. And what was given up *to,* was given back to us in a way that restored our Peace of mind, and the order in our lives.

The Willingness To Ask

We found that willingness was essential in going beyond our controloholism. We became willing to be shown another way. We found that we needed to ask, whether or not we called it prayer, a Power greater than ourselves to release us from our controloholism. We found, also, that if we had no willingness to give up our controls in a particular situation, we could *ask* for that willingness to be given. Our Higher Power had much willingness to give us, if we had none. We had only to ask. We found, if we were too full of fear to let go of our controls in a certain area, that our Higher Power could be asked to show us, beyond what we feared, to the safety of releasing our controls.

And, so, we asked for willingness, and we asked to be guided in our asking. We found that the only way to go beyond our controloholic addiction was to ask for another way and to be willing and open to having it shown.

Have you asked today?

Step One

"We admitted that we were powerless over control in our lives — that we could neither control nor manage our own lives."

To go beyond — we begin... one step at a time.

Step One

Step One is the point, where we finally come to the realization that our attempts at controlling do not work. It is a step we avoid, for we are very fearful of coming to this point. There is still a hope that our controls will work. But time and time again, we find they do not. It is a step where we finally see that our very attempts to control *are* the problem. Our wanting to control or manage any aspect of our lives is what has made our lives unmanageable. We, who have sought bigger and better controls, are at first very resistant to this step, for we have thought our controls, our managing, was what made our lives work for us. In this step, we finally see that what we have tried to control has never really worked. What we have tried to manage has always eluded us. The areas in which we have refused to let go, the areas we sought to control, are unmanageable.

When we finally admit, that it is our addiction to control in a given area that is the problem, then Step One becomes the point of great release. We have identified the problem, we have admitted it, and now we are ready for another way.

Does It Work Without Conflict?

*I don't like reading this checklist, when I'm trying to
control. It makes it impossible for me to be honest
about the list and to keep my controls at the same
time. Each time I'm into conflict, I'm asked by my
sponsor to read the list again. Needless to say,
by now I've gone through the checklist at least
a hundred times. I don't like having my controls
exposed but I know that when I'm willing to be honest
in reading this checklist, something releases in the
situation and a solution is always found.*

— Leanne

Any time we are into conflict, we are into trying to control
the situation. We are sometimes still under the belief that
managing to control works. But we ask ourselves this: *Does
it work without conflict?* We have thought that conflict, pain,
and sacrifice were natural components of getting anything
to work. We now realize: If there is any conflict — it is not
working. Peace is our goal and it is the Ease of Peace that we
will experience. Any other goal will have conflict. A conflict is a
sure sign we are doing things *our* way.

If we experience conflict, then in some area, we are managing
or trying to control.

A management checklist to see if we are trying to control:

What we try to control is always interfered with.

What we try to control is never listened to.

What we try to control is never appreciated.

What we try to control is always sabotaged.

What we try to control requires re-educating those around us.

What we try to control is surrounded by fools.

What we try to control always sees the difficulty as outside of ourselves.

What we try to control seeks agreement and alignment.

What we try to control seeks justification.

If we are sure our management works, we may ask ourselves: Does it work without conflict? Does conflict have anything to do with God's Peace?

Man Age Ment

We all have trouble letting go of the idea of our management. I was a teacher and my training was to "manage" a classroom of children. After all, I thought, if I didn't manage to keep those kids under control, surely there would be chaos. There had to be management somewhere.

Only now am I beginning to see that it isn't management itself that is the problem — it's my management rather than my Higher Power's management of any situation that brings difficulties. It's not that things don't get managed, it's that I need not take control of their management — I can let in God's management.

I heard a helpful definition of my ego management at a meeting. Ego was defined as: E dging G od O ut. My management or ego keeps God out — that's when my life becomes truly unmanageable. When I let go of my management, it's not that things aren't managed — it's that they are managed by my Higher Power's Wisdom, Love, and Understanding. When God is in my life, so much more is managed — but not by me.

— Leanne

No one will let go of anything unless they want to. This sounds very simplistic, but it is the first very important step in your journey Home.

You only give up that which you have no use for; for who would give up that for which he has a use?

The first step, then, is to realize — anything that does not bring you release, that does not bring you Peace, you do not want, for it has no use.

What we wish you to see is that you do not wish *your* management, you do not wish *your* control — it has no use for you.

Your management or trying to control only brings conflict.

It is when you see that anything you manage or try to control ultimately does not work, does not bring you Peace, then you will be willing to see *your* management has no use for you.

When you see *your* management is not useful, then you will be willing to admit — you cannot manage your life and be willing to give up your management, your control to your Higher Power.

It does not matter how noble your intentions are, if you attempt to manage or control anything, there will be separation and dis-ease.

It is not for you to manage; it is to have it managed by God.

It is in realizing you cannot manage anything that God's Peace may enter to heal and to provide a solution to the situation.

Truly admitting that you cannot manage alone is a realization that you are not alone and have the assistance of a Higher Power.

Admitting that you cannot manage or control anything is not to stress failure; it is to stress you cannot be without God.

You are given the gift of others who become barometers, whenever you are attempting to manage or control.

These people will faithfully reflect *your* management to the very degree of their resistance to you.

Understand, people are never attempting to sabotage *you* — they are always attempting to sabotage *your* management.

Your management will always say: "I'm in control here and you have to listen to me!" *Your* management as such is an attack and does not offer any real solutions.

You wish to be honest — to the degree you are willing to give up your management, your controls, will be your degree of honesty.

True honesty is fully realizing: "I, by myself, can manage nothing."

The more noble seem to be your intentions, the more you will try to manage or control. It does not matter — no goals, no matter how noble, will work, if you try to manage the outcome.

To see that you cannot manage your life, with your controls, is to join with others. To choose *your* management is to separate yourself from them.

To have your difficulties and conflicts resolved, you must want or desire to give up your management.

Your management is based entirely on judgment.

The only areas that can be healed are the ones you are willing to give up *your* management in.

Question: *So any form of dis-ease or dis-comfort will be our management or our attempt to control?*

Answer: *Yes. Even growing old or ultimately death is man age ment.*

What Do You Mean It Does Not Work?

In this book the word management is synonymous with control. I remember when I tried to prove that I could fix my bicycle through sheer will, control, and management. The harder I tried, the more pieces got scattered. I wound up very dirty with bruised knuckles. No way was I going to give in. After several hours, I was saved by sundown and darkness. When I stepped back from my management, and asked for the best to happen in God's time, the next morning saw the job easily completed in less than 10 minutes.
— Maynard

There is one thing you have not fully seen as yet, although it is very simple. It is simply this: *Whatever you try to manage does not get done.* The more you try to manage something, the less will be accomplished. So foreign is this to your thinking, that you have difficulty comprehending this statement. You still believe that the more you manage something, the more effective it will be.

Let us look at a few instances:

The more an alcoholic tries to manage staying sober, the more he will find himself drinking. The more you try to manage thinking of a name you have forgotten, the more it will elude you.

"Yes," you say, "But these are very simple examples and do not really apply to me!" Very well, we say. Let us see what applies to you. Let us take the area of business. Can you manage your business affairs? "Well, of course," you say, "How else is it to be done?" We say: Notice that in the times that you are managing business — how little business actually gets done? You frown in puzzlement and have to admit that in those times you are managing business, very little, if anything, gets done at all. But still, you shake your head, as if you are dreaming, and refuse to see that your management is the problem.

You still deny that your management is a problem. You still hold to the belief that it works and is necessary for anything to be accomplished. Let us shake this belief a little more.

When you manage writing a paper or a letter, does much get done, or do you end up spending your time pushing yourself or procrastinating doing the task? Do you spend time psyching yourself up, preparing yourself to begin? Do you spend endless hours postponing beginning, yet being "on call" until you begin? You may use a combination of the two; however, what we wish to point out is that your *management is* the waste of time.

"But what about my business contacts? Surely I have to manage forming and keeping these contacts?" First of all, let us say that when you are in the management position, you are on call 24 hours a day. It does not matter whether there are any contacts to be made at this moment — you are still on call. And as you are managing many things, you are on call all the time and can never really relax, nor can you be at Peace. What if a contact comes along and you are not prepared? If you are managing contacts, how can you relax and enjoy your life?

What we wish you to see is that when you are managing making contacts, all your time is spent on managing whether there are contacts or not. And more importantly, all the time you spend managing contacts interferes with having them made.

Consider: What if the contacts in your life had nothing to do with your management? What if they had everything to do with your willingness to have them made?

What we are really wanting you to see is that things may be done with Ease or with management. Management seems to accomplish things only because you work so hard managing. What we wish to show is that managing is an interference with what you want to accomplish, and, in all cases, actually prevents you from reaching the very thing you are attempting to manage.

"What about those things that I have accomplished through my management? Sometimes I have pushed and it has worked. Sometimes I have procrastinated and eventually got it done."

We say, yes — so it appears. But at what cost? Immediately that you speak of this, sacrifice enters the picture. At what cost do you push yourself? At what cost do you play the waiting game? With what "drug" do you keep yourself going? And what is the payment? Do you sacrifice your family, your happiness, your health, or your freedom? Which one has to go? And do you still think it is worth the price to be able to manage?

The denial that your management does not work is the greatest block to healing, to letting go. You still think somehow your management is still going to work. We ask you to see that whatever you manage will prevent you from the very thing you are asking for.

Finally admitting, that you cannot manage anything, is not a state of defeat — it is a state where you finally see, there is nothing that cannot be healed or accomplished. It is a state of finally seeing all that is loving, all that is best, is taken care of. It is not an inactive state — through your management you have been inactive and have wasted much time. How many hours have you procrastinated? How many hours have you sought to push yourself? How many hours have you sought to escape and recover from both?

It takes very little time to do anything. It takes no time at all for God's Will to be done. This is very active. It is active the very moment you ask and let It in. Your management is a state of much inactivity and is a waste of much time.

Your management does not work. It keeps you inactive and goes against the healing you wish to see.

It is time to see that your management *is* the difficulty, *is* the dis-ease, *is* the waste of time. How much does your management work? — Not at all.

I Want It My Way

I was not a problem drinker, I drank for solutions.
Although I don't like admitting this, I now see that
most of my problems have been caused by what I
have, at times, used for solutions — medications,
alcohol, drugs, arguing, fighting, force, fear, phobias,
depression, sickness, defensiveness, attack, blame,
guilt, denial, procrastination, pushing, avoidance...
just to name a few. The top of the list ought to be
— wanting my way.

— Maynard

There is one thing that you miss in the admittance of your
addiction. First of all, any goal, other than letting your Higher
Power run your life, becomes an addiction, because it is *your*
solution. We are, in a sense, addicted to *our* solutions rather
than *God's* solutions. What you fail to admit or see, when you
have an addiction, is that you are powerless in giving up this
addiction. You still want the addiction or solution to work.

Most alcoholics, when they come to the Program, finally come
because their solution of alcohol has made life unmanageable.
Usually, they come wanting to keep the solution, to learn how
to control it. They may say they want to give up drinking but
really they would like to keep the solution, if only it did not
make life so desperate.

The same applies to any addiction or anything that is used
as our solution. Healing does not take place, until we finally
admit we are powerless over any desire or willingness to give
up this solution. In other words — we still want our goal or

solution to work. We are powerless to give up wanting this goal ahead of Peace. The truth is — we don't want another way, because this solution or goal has been chosen above all else.

The first step must include the knowledge, that without God's help, we are powerless in even wanting another way. *We cannot manage our addiction, nor can we manage our compulsion to keep this addiction.*

If there is still conflict after we have taken Step One, then we must realize we have not admitted our deep attachment to *our* goal, to *our* solution, to *our* addiction. The A.A. Program says: "Without help it is too much for us." Truly even the choosing of the goal of Sobriety or Peace is too much for us, without God's help. Our powerlessness lies in our inability to let go of *our* goals in order to choose Peace or Sanity.

Once we admit we cannot let go of these goals — we have tried but it has been too much for us — then we can see the full extent of our powerlessness without God's help. We are not asked to let go of our goals. We are only asked to admit our powerlessness in letting them go, so Sanity may be given to us.

We do not restore ourselves to Sanity — our Higher Power does. If we could restore ourselves to Sanity, we would have done so.

All our solutions are an attempt to do something on our own. This is a state of Power-lessness. Being Power-less is being without the knowledge of our Higher Power.

Before any healing can take place, it is to admit we still want our old solutions; we still want to hold on to them. Even knowing there is another way makes no difference, we are Power-less by ourselves to choose it. We are Power-less even over a willingness to choose it. Once we admit this powerlessness and ask God to provide another way, to assist us in our choice and to give us the willingness to make it, healing takes place. By the Grace of God, we are released from our addiction.

"Probably no human power could help us choose another way or relieve us of our addiction."

We admit we are powerless over our choice of goals, other than Peace. We admit we are still holding onto these goals, but we would like the willingness to truly desire another way.

Prayer:

Yes, I would like another way but I still want my way above all else. I can't seem to let go of it — God help me.

Amen

At Long Lost

Question: *How do I begin, when I'm not sure whether I come from management or not? I don't want to begin, when I'm into trying to control.*

Answer: *If you are asking this question, you are into management of whether or not you are into management. It is not up to you to stop managing or trying to control before you begin. Simply begin and ask God to look after your management.*

It is the same as saying: You are only lost if you are trying to find the way. Many people will not begin, until they feel they know the way. We say: Begin by admitting you do not know the way, but you are willing to let God show you the way.

The best way to get lost is to put yourself in charge of finding the direction.

I Already Gave At The Office

So, you have finally taken Step One. You have admitted your life is unmanageable and that you cannot manage anything. "I have admitted this," you complain, "and still things are not as they should be. I have admitted I cannot manage anything and still nothing is happening!"

You wonder why you procrastinate when you have taken Step One. You have admitted you cannot manage anything - so what are you procrastinating for? You've admitted you could not manage your life, but you still find yourself pushing for results. If you have really taken Step One, what is the difficulty?

Let us look at how you have taken Step One. It sounds something like this: "I will admit I cannot manage my life *until* such time that I can manage it." What you are really saying is that you don't have it together right now, but wait a while!

We ask you to look closely at Step One again. Is there anything that says you admit the unmanageability of your life, only until you can manage it? Step One clearly states that our life is unmanageable — period. It does not state, that at some future time, you will be able to manage it. Step One is a realization that your life will not work without God in *everything* that you do. You don't admit unmanageability in order to get it together at some future time. You admit this in order to see that your life, without God, will always be unmanageable. It is a realization that somewhere along the way, you have lost your connection with God and it is this disconnection that makes life impossible to manage by you. It is a realization that by yourself, your life will always be unmanageable. It is an opening for God to enter. It is saying: "Your Way, not my way, works here."

Step One is as true today as it will be tomorrow. By yourself, you will not be able to manage tomorrow either.

We invite you to take Step One in all areas of your life and at all times in your life.

Step Two

"We came to believe that a Power greater than ourselves could restore us to sanity."

We go beyond our controls, to find that Power within ourselves which is everything, and that connects us with all things.

Step Two

For those of us brought up in conventional religion, this is the step we have great resistance to. In some instances, we have been taught that God is a vengeful being, punishing us for our wickedness. We have suffered much guilt and much fear in our dealings with the Higher Power of our teachings. We find that we have difficulty trusting in the notion of a Higher Power. In fact, the main reason we have sought to control with such intensity is that we had lost all faith or respect for the God of our upbringing, for the God as we had understood Him. Now we find, we must call upon the very Power we have so long neglected or resisted. It is indeed a dilemma for, in many cases, the very Power we must have faith in, we have lost all faith for.

But in this step, we are only asked to *consider* that there may be a Power greater than ourselves that could assist us at this time. We are asked to open to a Power that is loving enough to forgive whatever we have done, or continue to do, in order to bring us another way.

This step is a consideration step. It is a consideration that God and others may actually be there for us. We may even ask God to show us beyond all our misperceptions that we hold about Him, in order for us to see His loving guidance. We ask for the God, of our *loving* understanding, to guide us now. We let Him look after all the misperceptions that we have been taught and perhaps still believe about Him. In this consideration, we invite the awareness of a Higher Power that can restore us to sanity and bring order back into whatever area we have sought to control.

Came To Believe

One of my favorite obsessions was trying to figure out why my life was so miserable; why I did the things I did; why I felt the way I did; why I said the things I did. Then I was told: "You can't make sense out of insanity." That made it simple — coming from using my controls was insane and I wasn't ever going to figure anything out in that state, because while I was controlling, I was insane. It isn't up to me to figure out the insanity in my life, but it is up to me to ask to see Sanity. It's a simple change of focus.

— Leanne

You are only crazy, when you do not recognize the insanity of *your* thinking.

Sanity is not of you, so there is no need to maintain it. Simply by questioning your own sanity, you are in a position to ask for the sanity of healing. Beginning to question your own sanity, is the first step in healing.

If you are responsible for your own sanity, then be assured, you are quite insane.

Insane simply means: Trying to maintain a reality separate from God's.

If things begin to look crazy, you are not responsible for making sanity out of the insane. All that is required is that you ask that you see Peace and healing even here. The healing *you* bring is to ask for healing to occur. In this you need do nothing.

You may ask: "Let me see Your Healing or Will done here."

Where Is The Switch?

Rather than focusing on powerlessness, which is quite fearful, the question really is: "Where is the Power?"

When you finally admit you are in darkness and don't know how to stop seeking darkness, then the next question is: "Where is the Light? Where is the Power?"

Truly, all powerlessness means is operating without Power. Rather than this being fearful, it is an opportunity to ask The Power to come into our lives. If you are in darkness, do you curse it or do you ask to see Light? Do you fear your state of Power-lessness or being without Power, or in this state do you ask for Power to be given? — the Power of Love, the Power of Acceptance, the Power of God.

This admittance of being without Power and asking for the Power to be given is the Light switch or the 180 degree turn.

It is asking for Light, rather than focusing on being without power, that is the solution.

Dependency

To reach a state of perfect Peace and Love, complete dependency is required. You must depend on your Higher Power for everything. You must depend on His solutions, His Will above all else: "Thou shalt have no other dependencies before Me."

If you depend on a career for happiness, you will be left unfulfilled. If you depend on wealth for your safety, you will be left feeling bereft and empty. If you depend on another for love and support, you will be left feeling unloved and alone. If you depend on drugs or alcohol for your connection to life, you will be left feeling disconnected from everything.

There is only One you may depend upon. If you place your dependency on anything else, you are worshipping an idol that cannot support you.

If you think you can depend on a bank account, you will fear loss. If you think you can depend on an enterprise, you will be resentful if this is not attained. If you think you can depend on a relationship for your completeness, you will feel weak and continuously suspicious.

To know the Peace of God, you must be willing to depend on God for everything. As you cannot manage your lives alone, you can depend on nothing outside of God; for there *is* nothing outside of God. *Dependence on anything else will not bring you happiness.*

Depending on God does not mean you dictate the terms; it means you also depend on Him to determine what is best for you. This is the dependency of surrender or joining.

You must depend on God to heal all relationships. You must depend on God for all that would sustain you. You must depend on God for all direction. This dependency is opening — opening to let God's Power finally guide your every step.

On this one thing you may depend: In being willing to depend on the Peace of God as being your one goal, all solutions will be given.

You will be at Peace, when you depend on God for all things.

Dependence Day

*The fact that I was still smoking did not deter me from giving advice (add-vice) to a friend of mine preoccupied with the thoughts of quitting smoking. While indulging ourselves in analyzing, I could see his rebellious nature and motives for starting smoking, and where smoking had been used by him to keep a sense of autonomy, a "proof" of growing up. I thank him for being my mirror by showing me that I, too, started smoking as a perverse declaration of independence, steeped in an adolescent mentality. Although I craved smoking, I never really liked it. The irony is that in seeking independence through smoking, I created a dependency on nicotine. **In my deep desire for Freedom, I had confused independence with Freedom.** I see I'm not alone in this. Two weeks after our conversation, on the 4th of July, I quit smoking. Now the 4th of July is my Freedom Day, not Independence Day.*

— Maynard

You are proud of your independence. You are proud of the fact that you can do many things by yourself. There are a few areas to be ironed out, but eventually you hope to be entirely independent in these areas also. You are dependent on "nobody for nothin". Well — almost nobody. Hopefully this too shall pass. Independence Day is your favorite holiday. It is something you aspire to with all your being.

While you hold this perception, we come along and suggest you become totally dependent on God for everything. You don't like this suggestion. In fact, you find it outrageous and resist it with all the indignity at your command. Dependence — any kind of dependence — is totally opposite to the direction you have been going. Dependence, you think, is the cause of difficulties, not their solution.

Surely we are totally mistaken here. This may be so; however, we invite you to question your belief of dependence. Perhaps in this belief *you* have been mistaken.

First of all, dependence is not a four- letter word, although you have sought to make it so. Dependence on God is the gateway to your freedom and the passage Home.

You are not required to become dependent on another's beliefs or misperceptions. You are not required to compromise your integrity in order to rely on another's illusions. What you are required to do, is to become willing to see that you may be dependent on your Higher Power healing all relationships, solving all difficulties, and bringing Peace to any situation. This is the dependence we would invite you to consider.

Truly, your struggle for independence has been a resistance against having to "buy" another's illusion. You thought that if you were to become dependent on anyone, you would have to accept beliefs you knew to be untrue. You thought dependence meant a trade-off. "I'll be dependent on you, and in this dependence I will have to accept everything that you say and do to be true."

You see dependence as a sacrifice you must make in order to be supported by anyone or anything. That is why you treasure independence so much, for you think it buys you the right to keep your integrity without compromise. You believe that if you become dependent, you forfeit any kind of choice. In short — you lose your freedom.

You feel that if you are dependent, you will be in a position of being totally controlled by whatever or whoever you are dependent on. If you become dependent, then you must pay for any kind of service or support with your deepest integrity. Thus you resolve — it is a matter of integrity or compromise. Seen in this light, or lack thereof, you choose integrity and independence.

The one thing you may have noticed with independence is that you can never totally let yourself be helped or supported by anyone. To be independent, you have to do everything yourself; otherwise, you may become dependent on another.

Even your prayers to God, are a request for His strength in order for you to become more independent — "Please give me Your strength, so that I may do this myself."

Thus, you become dependent on yourself for all means of support. All prayers become requests to allow you more ways of supporting yourself. Indeed, you have many tensions and reminders not to become dependent on anyone; not to let in any support, except that which you can generate or determine, will not make you dependent.

Support, other than that which you can provide yourself, is viewed with much suspicion. You tend to keep it out first and ask questions later.

We would wish to give you another way of seeing dependence:

This way of seeing involves no compromise.
It would let in all support.
It would respect integrity.
It would judge nothing.
It would involve the support of all things.

This dependence is a free choice,
And would ask nothing in return — no sacrifice.
It would only ask that you consider being dependent,
On a Source that would show you another way,
That would show you Peace,
That would show you Healing.

This Source asks that you be dependent on Its Love,
To gently remove all resistance,
And to gently let in,
The innocence of others.
This dependence only requires a little willingness,
To have the Peace of each moment,
And the support that is all around,
Shown to you.

This dependence would show you the support,
That is all around you,
The guidance that is always there,
And the Joy that is yours.
It would show you an end,
To all conflict and pain.

You are not required to believe anything,
That you do not feel in your heart,

To be true.
You are not required to depend on illusions,
Only on loving direction.

There is nothing to give.
There is nothing to sell.
There is only a grateful acceptance of this
dependence,
Which would lift all burdens from you.
And there is only a giving,
That comes from this dependence,
In order to pass on all the support,
That you are maintained with.

Let this dependence through;
For with it, comes all of the support of others,
And of God.
This dependence would not hold you,
But would encourage you to give,
As you have received —
In openness and in Peace.

Step Three

"We made a decision to turn our will and our lives over to the care of God as we understood Him."

Although things may appear to be falling apart, maybe for the first time, they are falling together.

Step Three

Step Three is the decision step. It is not a step where a lot is required of us; it is a step where we are asked to make a decision. Once we make this decision — the decision to turn our will and our lives over to the care of God — the rest is taken care of for us.

Our will has meant a life built on controls. We finally come to a point, where we realize our will has led nowhere. This is where, we make a decision for another way — God's Way. It is a point, where we finally decide — "Anything is better than the controlled life I am leading."

For many of us, the concept of God still poses a stumbling block. In some cases, we find it is easier to say: "God as I *don't* understand Him." Because we carry many misunderstandings about God, about a Higher Power, it has helped many of us to consider God as "*G*ood *O*rderly *D*irection." We, in the midst of chaos and control, want so much the direction and guidance of a loving God.

We make a decision, despite our fears, to let God run our lives, where we have tried to control. We make a decision to ask for God's help in dealing with whatever problems surround us. In short, we make a decision to ask for help. We have tried to do it on our own, but our controls have only brought pain. We make a decision that God will run our lives from now on, and we make a decision to have Him show us how to continually turn our lives over to Him. All we have to do is make a decision, and even in this, we can ask for God's help.

We make a decision, and God is there to help us turn our will and lives over to His care.

Beyond

We trust not that God will manage to keep our worst fears from happening; we trust that God will show us beyond our worst fears.

So, we do not ask God: "Please don't let me fail!" We ask: "God, please show me beyond success and failure."

"God please use anything that happens on this journey for healing."

A Void Dance

Your life has been one long avoidance. Indeed, if your goal
is not to let go, let God, then it is avoidance of one form or
another. *Your* goals are to avoid. You choose goals that would
avoid pain, discomfort. You choose goals that would avoid
loss; that would avoid death; that would avoid fear. All your
goals are chosen to avoid what you do *not* want. You are very
clear on what you do *not* want, and these things you seek
to avoid.

You avoid confrontations; you avoid being still; you avoid
being in the moment; you avoid looking within; but most of all,
you avoid letting go to God. You avoid these things because
you fear loss of control. You fear, if you let go, all those things
you have avoided will come, without any ability on your part
to control them.

What you do not see is that you have been doing a-void-dance.
You have sought to fill the void, where you have not let God
into your life.

Understand, when you are managing anything, you will be
into avoidance; you will be avoiding the flow; you will be
dancing around the void left by keeping God out.

When you are into avoidance, you focus on those things which
you fear, and thus you keep them. If you are avoiding loss,
you keep the belief in loss. If you are avoiding pain, you keep
the belief in pain. If you are avoiding insecurity, you will keep
the belief in insecurity.

The solution is not to confront your fears, for this also keeps the belief. Confrontation is also a-void-dance, for it would still avoid the solution of letting God in. Rather than avoid or confront your fears, we ask you to change your focus. If you fear death, it is not to avoid the thought or confront it — it is to choose *Life*. If you fear illness and pain, it is not to avoid or confront — it is to choose *Wholeness*. It is not to avoid or confront your feelings of lack — it is to ask to see *Support*. As you see, all of the focuses we have given you are simply other names for God. It is not to avoid or confront your difficulties — it is to ask to be with *Ease*.

If you are into avoidance, then you are relying on *your* solutions and your solutions will always leave "a void" around which you will continue to dance.

> *Our sponsor had already shown me that it was not letting go to Love that I feared, but rather I feared the loss of controls that unconditional Love would dissolve. To go beyond my juvenile and fearful connotations that I had projected onto the word "God," our sponsor often used other words that, in their unconditional sense, would also denote God. Our sponsor said that another name for God is Love. Another name for God is Peace. Another name for God is Life, Trust, Support, Ease, Joy, Higher Power, Now, Innocence, Grace, Mercy, Great Spirit, Oneness, Truth, Happiness... and so on. Rather than God being my narrow and limited experience of this word, I can now see God is all these things and so much more.*
> — *Maynard*

I Can't Handle Any More

At various times in your day, you reach a point where you conclude: "This is all I can handle!" Once you reach this point, you will prevent anything else from encroaching on this space. You say hotly in defense: "This is all I can handle, don't give me anything more or I'll crack under the strain." If anyone insists on giving you more than what you feel you can handle, you have developed powerful defenses to prevent them going any further — you either get sick or very tired; you either feel manipulated or put upon; you either get angry or retreat completely into a strong shell. All of these defenses say to the world: "Don't come in any closer. This is all I'm prepared to handle!"

From this, it appears that the world is making you tired or feel manipulated; sick or cut off. We say it is time you saw that these feelings are feelings *you* activate; defenses you erect, when the world gives you "more than you can handle". Can you not see that you are the one deciding what you should be handling? No one gave you anything to handle; you chose that responsibility yourself. You think the world demands much of you. Truly, it is the world *as you perceive it* that demands much of you. It is your perception that demands you handle anything. There is only One Who can handle anything. He has not asked you to handle any situation. He has only asked that you be willing to let Him take care of any concern you may have, if you simply give it to Him.

You say that Alcoholics Anonymous tells you: "God only gives you as much as you can handle." If you truly look at your First Step, you will see this is not the Twelve Step Program; for the First Step asks you to admit that your life, with your handling

of it, is unmanageable. God does not ask you to handle
anything. Your function is only to become more and more
willing to let Him handle all aspects of your life. Can you not
see, it is your determination to handle anything that makes
the world seem too demanding; that makes your barriers and
defenses seem necessary — all the tiredness, all the feelings of
manipulation, all dis-ease?

When there is nothing to handle, there is nothing to keep out,
and your feelings of loneliness and frustration disappear. It
is time you see that you are the one keeping out the support
and closeness of those around you; you are the one perceiving
demands that are more than you can bear. And it is time to
see, all that you think you can handle must be given to God so
you may feel the freedom of being at one with all things.

> Maynard's daughter was getting married. With family
> members present from his two previous marriages, it
> could be considered an awkward situation. We were
> both getting tense trying to make everything smooth
> between each other and those around us. Maynard
> felt like he was living in cotton batting and I, too, felt
> numb and disconnected.
>
> Finally, our sponsor pointed out the difference
> between making things smooth and allowing God to
> look after the situation. Making things smooth was
> still **our** solution and was conditional on everything
> going without any disturbance. When we allowed
> God to look after the situation, then anything could be
> used by Him for healing. Maynard listened and then
> complained that he still felt there was something he
> should be looking after. Our sponsor said, "Okay,"

and had me find a chunk of metal and give it to
Maynard. He said that all Maynard had to do was
look after the piece of metal and his Higher Power
would take care of the rest — the relatives, the
wedding... everything.

At first, Maynard was tremendously relieved and
it looked like a fair deal to me. It seemed so simple
— all he had to handle was two ounces of metal.
Then the serious questions came. Where should he
keep the metal? What if he lost it? Should he keep
it by him when he slept? What if it fell out when
he was walking his daughter down the aisle? That
small piece of metal began to drive him crazy. The
management of it obsessed him.

Then our sponsor returned and asked how the metal
management was going. Maynard complained that
he hadn't realized how managing a small piece of
metal could grow into such a difficult problem. Our
sponsor gently pointed out that anything we try to
manage soon gets out of control. He reminded us that
we give **everything** to our Higher Power to look after,
that even the tiniest management soon overwhelms
our lives.

It was such a valuable lesson to us, for anytime we
think there is some small part of our lives we can
manage, we remember that tiny piece of metal and
realize that it isn't the size of what we are trying to
control that is the difficulty; it is the management of
anything that makes our lives miserable.

— Leanne

The Tiny Step

You still do not see the tiny step you must take to come Home. You are still trying to turn your life and will over to the care of God. This is not necessary. Simply be *WILLING* to have your life and will turned over to the *Care* of God and with this choice *He* will do the rest.

But How Do You Do That?

You assume that being in control gives you a choice. We say: You only assume control, when you don't see there is a choice. You think: "I have no choice; therefore, I better control the situation." Only when you see that you truly do have a choice, will you also see control is not necessary. If you truly have a choice, then you give up control, or in giving up control, do you see you truly have a choice.

You have many books on how to do things — *How to Win Friends and Influence People, How to Succeed Without Really Trying,* how to start living, how to start loving, how to raise children, how to write a paper, how to lose weight, how to be spiritual... You are obsessed with having to know how to do something. In most cases, if you don't know how, you will not begin. "Tell me how to do this so I can get started. I don't know how to do this — so I won't begin." Does this sound familiar?

You feel stuck because you do not know *how* to live. You don't know *how* to be spiritual. "I just don't know how!" Your goal in everything is to know how, and you don't believe anything can be accomplished until you know how it is to be accomplished.

We say to you: Let go, let God. You say: "I don't know how." We say: Ask for a little willingness. You say: "How do you do this? Give me the right formula, the right process, the right procedure. How can I let go, let God when I don't know how?"

You believe that you can do nothing, or nothing can be accomplished, without you knowing how. Knowing how is a prerequisite for everything you do, everything you ask for. "I won't do this or ask for that because I do not know how it is to be accomplished."

We ask you a very fundamental question: What if *your* knowing how was not necessary to having anything accomplished? You look stunned — "How can that be? How can that happen? How can you say something like that?"

The point is, the condition that you know how to do something before you ask or begin, is a condition that prevents accomplishment. Having to know how is a block to having Peace, to having Abundance, to having God's Guidance in your Life. It says: "I cannot go on until I know how."

We ask you to consider: What if knowing how was not needed? What if you admitted you did not know how things were to be accomplished, but that you were open to whatever way was appropriate for them to be accomplished?

Immediately the word "how?" is on the tip of your tongue. Again we say: What if you did not have to know how? What if you could ask anyway? What if you could begin, open to having these things accomplished, open to having these requests facilitated *even if you didn't know how?* What we would have you see is that having to know how blocks the natural flow. It limits many possibilities and opportunities by saying: "It is not possible until I know how."

You say: "How can I do what is of value to me? How can I follow my Integrity, when I don't know how it is to be accomplished?" We say: What does knowing how have to do with anything? *Simply begin by admitting you do not know how, but you would like to see certain things accomplished anyway.* Do you know how to stay sober? You have to admit, you do not. But in this admittance, in asking God to help you stay sober, in choosing Sobriety — it is accomplished.

So you do not know how. Are you willing to be shown? Are you willing to choose anyway? So you don't know how it is to be accomplished. Are you willing to ask and consider it taken care of, even if you don't know how it is to be done?

What if knowing how was not necessary? What if you could open to all the possibilities, all the many ways something could be accomplished by saying: "I choose God's Peace anyhow; I choose Integrity anyhow; I choose to ask for all that disturbs me, all that troubles me, all that I want to do, all that I want accomplished, all that I want looked after, to be done anyhow — even if I don't know how it is to be done."

It is time to limit yourselves no longer; it is time to say:

> **"I don't know how, but it still may be accomplished.**
>
> **I don't know how, but You do.**
>
> **I don't know how, but I would like to see it anyway.**
>
> **I don't know how, but I am willing to begin.**
>
> **I don't know how, but I am willing to choose.**
>
> **I don't know how, but I am willing to be shown.**
>
> **I don't know how, but I am open to the possibility.**
>
> **I don't know how — You do — Please show me."**
>
> **Amen**

It isn't to pretend that you know how; it is to say you don't know how, but you are open to the best way to see things accomplished.

Truly, in choosing Peace, in choosing what is loving, we automatically know how; we automatically know what is appropriate. However, the how does not come first — the choice for Peace, the choice for Wellness, the choice for Joy does.

> *When my sponsor spoke of giving up my knowing to have my Higher Power's knowing, I interpreted that to mean everything I had learned to date was useless. I was very discouraged, for here I had painstakingly acquired a university education, courses, methods, tools, techniques and exercises for counselling people. And now, I thought, I couldn't use anything anymore — all my knowledge was down the drain.*
>
> *In the midst of my discouragement, my sponsor gently pointed out that when we give up our knowing to God, it isn't to discard it — it is rather that God can use anything we give Him for healing. He can use my university degree, my tools and my methods. He can even use my lack of knowledge, if I just trust in His solutions. In other words, I don't have to know, I will be given knowing. All I have learned is still useful, but I don't control the use — God does.*
>
> *My tools, my learning no longer comes first — the guidance of my Higher Power does. My sponsor told me that we are not healed by methods, we are healed by God working through these methods. He told me that we don't put the methods first — we put*

*God first. All that I know may be used by my Higher
Power, and in putting Him first, the appropriate
words, the appropriate tools can then be given.*
                                                    — Leanne

One Moment Please!

You are still thinking of letting go in terms of time. You think of turning your will and life over as being forever. You have difficulty turning your life over to the care of God for this length of time — it is incomprehensible to you.

We say, you still think of forever as being connected with time. Forever to you deals only with the future. You cannot see how you can possibly let go that long.

We say — are you willing to turn your life and will over to the care of God this moment — not forever — but for this moment? Realize, you can only let go NOW — in this moment.

Can you manage your life this moment? Is there One Who can this moment? Are you willing to let go of your will this moment? Are you willing to ask for guidance this moment? That is all — just for this moment.

There is only the Eternal Now. You are not asked to let go forever, you are asked to let go NOW.

Take Care

We will speak on care. If someone tells you to take care, in your mind it means an added responsibility. If you were to take care in your work or with a particular project, it would seem that more effort was required. This extra effort would not be welcomed by you. So there is a reluctance to take care in many things you do. "If I were to take care in all the areas I needed to take care in, I would be totally overwhelmed and exhausted."

Let us see where Care comes from. If *you* take care, then indeed anything you do is an effort. If you take or receive the Care of God, then anything you do can be done with Ease. When we say: Take Care, we do not mean to add more responsibility to you. We really mean — would you take the Gift of God's Care?

Prayer

God, would you give me Your Care
So that I may give the Care
That is needed in whatever I do.

My care takes effort,
Your Care is what accomplishes
All that is healing and loving.

My care becomes cares or worries,
Your Care becomes Ease and Peace.
Please take my cares and give me
Your Care instead.

It is not that I do not care;
It is that I let Your Care be given,
I let Your Care enter.

In all that I would accomplish,
Would You give me Your Care,
So that I would not have to just get by,
But with Your Care,
Each task may be done in the most
appropriate way,
And to the fullest of Your Creativity.

Let each thing I do be filled with Your Care,
So that there may be care and caring,
In whatever I do.

Amen

The Foundation

This is a daily program. We follow the steps daily. Each day and in every situation where we find conflict, we admit that we have been trying to control; and consequently, as a result of our trying to control, the day or the situation has become unmanageable.

We then ask for the Sanity of a Higher Power to enter our day and the particular situation in which we are disturbed.

We make a decision on a daily basis, on a moment-to-moment basis, to turn our day and each situation over to the Care of God, as we are coming to understand Him.

We become willing to let the first three steps run our lives. Our lives are now built on this solid foundation. Many Twelve Step Programs summarize these three steps thusly:

"I can't.

God can.

Let Him."

Step Four

"We made a searching and fearless moral inventory of ourselves."

Our goal is not to seek for darkness, our purpose is to bring forth any darkness we find, so that the Light of our Higher Power may dissolve it.

Step Four

Step Four is when we finally take stock of all the things we have been holding on to. This includes not only our resentments and our grievances, but it also includes those qualities in ourselves which we would like to see grow and develop. Our lives did not work because we had tried to manage them. The more we tried to manage, the more resentments and the more grievances we carried.

In this step, we make a list of all our resentments, grievances and any part of our lives that has been unforgiving. We make a list of all the manipulations we have used, all our attempts to control, all those areas we have sought to manage. We write about our anger and frustrations. We write about what we thought had been done to us. We take stock of what is hurting in our lives — what we have not let go of.

But in any stock-taking, we also look for the value. We look for that in our lives, in our being, which has brought Peace, which has brought us closer to others and ourselves. We seek and write about those qualities in ourselves which we appreciate and wish to see grow. We make a list of qualities that we would like in our lives, that we would like to see developed and nurtured.

This is the step where we look at what we have been holding on to. And whether we have been holding on to something that brings us pain or something that brings us release, we realize it is *the holding on to* that has caused us difficulty. We realize that anything we have sought to use has been destructive for us.

This is a preparation step. We prepare a list of what we have been managing in order to share it and in order to turn it over. Our stock-taking eliminates nothing. Whether we try to manage our defects or our God-given gifts — it is still management. We prepare our stock for a new Manager. We bring out everything so God may use it or dissolve it. We have a look at our "business" and then prepare to give over our management, our control.

We can indeed afford to do this fearlessly, because it is not a matter of judging the inventory; it is a matter of seeing what works and what does not; what blocks us and what sets us free. And it is a matter of turning over, even what works, to God for His management.

It is an inventory of our lives and of our choices. It is not a step of blame or guilt — it is a step of release. It is a step of cleansing, and it is a step that makes an entirely new beginning possible. It is a step that will allow us to both forgive and be forgiven. It is a step that allows us to leave all our useless baggage behind. It is a step of freedom. It is a step that shows us beyond what we have made to who we really are. It is a step that puts us in touch with ourselves. It is a step that allows us to come empty-handed to each other and to God.

Using Or What's The Use?

What we use, uses us. We only use in order to control or manipulate. An alcoholic uses alcohol for many different reasons, but the main reason is to control feelings of pain, anxiety, and fear.

We use many things to control, but whatever we use, uses us. Whatever we use, for any reason, uses us. Whether we use guilt, anger, silence, being upset, ignoring, leaving, sarcasm, humour, walls... these things all use us. We become controlled by that which we use to control.

A list of some of the things we "use".

— intellectualizing — expertise

— gravity or seriousness — anger/displeasure

— being easily offended — shouting

— knowing better — discouragement

— the past — being unfulfilled — pouting

— giving up on

— resignation/washing our hands of

— religion/belief — being divinely guided

— teaching lessons — changing the subject

— throwing things — commotions, temper

— putdowns and corrections — criticism

— being busy — not having enough time

— superiority — inferiority — weakness

— sickness — procrastination — pushing

— being disappointed — being bored

— comparisons — tit for tat, revenge, getting even

— doing "own" thing — not getting caught up

— keeping a distance — complaining

— motivating and helping others

— not giving a straight answer

— embarrassment — being betrayed

— being tired — self-pity — guilt trip

— gross-outs — crying — making fun of

— unhappiness — doing something "drastic"

— running, quitting... life is over

— special occasions — contacts — being a victim

— pointing out — sensationalism — shock

— phobias — excuses — denial — importance

— smiles (smugness) — force

— needing someone or something — sex

— niceness — pleasing — flattery — bribes — money

— drugs, alcohol, eating, emotions, gambling, shopping...

What we use, we must keep in order to use. If you wonder why so many unpleasant things are in your life, ask yourself, "Am I using them?"

The question is: Are you happy? If not, the question is: What are you using?"

What we deny cannot be healed.

Seeing only what another uses will not bring *you* healing. It is to finally admit what you have been using.

> *It is helpful whenever I am caught up in anger or depression to have my sponsor remind me that I am "using". He tells me, "Rather than saying you are angry or depressed right now, say you are "using" anger or depression at this moment." To admit that I am using something as a solution, gives me a choice. As long as I think I am my anger, I won't see my choice. As long as I think using anger gets me somewhere, I won't want to let it go. But if I see it as another of my controlling solutions to get my way, then I can ask for another solution — my Higher Power's solution.*

> *I remember I was very discouraged one day. My sponsor asked — "Why are you using discouragement?" At first I was offended, because I thought I was "genuinely" discouraged. But then I asked for the honesty to look at my use of discouragement, and I saw that I was using being discouraged so others in my life would take over and fix things my way. It was my signal to God and the rest of the world that because I was discouraged, things had better go my way. I thought only drug addicts "used" but I found "using" was an appropriate term to describe my controloholism.*

Rather than getting discouraged or using discouragement, I can ask for help, without having to con anyone with my discouragement.

It is the same when I use sadness. Sometimes I use it so others will do what I want them to. The only problem, my sponsor points out, is that I have to stay sad in order to use sadness. Sometimes sadness comes and that's okay too. I can accept the feeling and ask my Higher Power to show me another way of seeing beyond my sadness. But I can tell when I'm using, because what I'm using doesn't go away. I've invested in its use rather than giving it to my Higher Power.

I am not the things I use. I am not anger, or depression, or confusion, or even niceness, because these are all things I've used to control. When I stop using, I'm real. The feelings and actions that come are real. What is real for me isn't what I use, it's what my Higher Power gives me, what being with my Higher Power lets me be, when I give all my uses to Him.

— Leanne

Exceptions To Honesty

To all of *your* rules there are exceptions. In the matter of honesty, there can be no exceptions. Either you are honest and open or you are not. You have sought to create exceptions to being totally honest. Here are a few:

It's okay to be dishonest with authority — government, police, and so on.

It's okay to be dishonest if it can avoid getting you in trouble.

It's okay to be dishonest with someone who has hurt or betrayed you in any way.

It's okay to be dishonest if you are trying to please someone.

It's okay to be dishonest if you are trying to impress someone or promote something.

It's okay to be dishonest when nobody is looking. (What they can't see can't hurt them.)

It's okay to be dishonest when you think honesty might hurt someone's feelings.

It's okay to be dishonest when you are making a point.

It's okay to be dishonest when your survival is at stake.

It's okay to be dishonest to keep someone's love, to avoid someone's anger.

It's okay to be dishonest in order to get even.

It's okay to be dishonest in order to be successful.

It's okay to be dishonest in order to avoid pain.

It's okay to be dishonest in order to look good.

It's okay to be dishonest in order to manage time more effectively.

It's okay to be dishonest in order to get out of something.

It's okay to be dishonest in order to teach a lesson.

It's okay to be dishonest in order to get what you want.

It's okay to be dishonest in order to serve a good cause.

Remember this: Dishonesty is only necessary, when you are relying on your own strength. If you think you must be in charge of anything, you must be dishonest in order to do so. Dishonesty is simply keeping back or hiding the truth. You wish things to go a certain way, and to have it so, you make your "truth". When you finally realize that your Higher Power may use anything for healing, then honesty becomes possible. We leave the Truth to Him and become willing to open to others. This is honesty. It is starting where you are and asking your Higher Power for His reinterpretation of all things. It is saying: "I really don't know what is best but I wish the best to be done. Please show me."

Get The Point?

We like pointing out what needs to be fixed in others. It is one of our favorite past times. But we begin to realize that when we are pointing out to others, we fail to see what is needed to be admitted in our own lives — we fail to point in.

Sometimes the actions of those around us cause us great annoyance. "What is the matter with them? Why do they do that? I wish they would change or stop what they are doing!"

We have come to see the value of observing what disturbs us in others. Rather than trying to point out or fix them, we realize that their actions are really a gift to us in assisting us to do our own inventory. It is a reflective universe, for anything that disturbs us in another, is what we have not looked at in ourselves. What we see reflected in another is part of our own inventory in one form or another. Those around us are our mirrors, and sometimes we do not like what we see in our mirror.

Rather than resisting or trying to fix our mirrors, we may use this reflection to do our own inventory. Those around us will assist us in taking stock of our own lives. We may fight this, or we may see this as an opportunity to let go of what we have hidden and what continues to disturb us. We're no longer interested in pointing out, for our journey would go within to our own healing, our own admittance.

I Should Be Doing...

There are many things you think you should be doing but are not. The list is endless. And each time you say: "I should be doing something but I am not," a little more guilt is added to your collection. You carry much guilt concerning all the things you should be doing but are not. And the more you think of all the things you should be doing, the more guilty you become. It does not matter whether you can possibly do all the things you think you should be doing at the same time — you continue to insist you should be doing them.

After a while, you have so many things you think you should be doing but are not that the burden of guilt you carry weighs you down completely. You become incapacitated — incapacitated with the guilt and fear you carry. Even the most simple things become a horrendous task that you cannot face doing. You are afraid even to move for fear the strain will destroy you. Everywhere you look, you see things you should be doing but are not. In your insane way of solving this problem, you ease the guilt by creating an excuse of sickness or even death. For with all the things you should be doing and are not, life becomes unbearable and death is seen as an escape from your burden.

Add to this already heavy burden — all the things you should *be* and are not — and you can begin to understand why a simple request for honesty seems so terrifying. For you believe honesty is admitting all the things you should be *doing* and are not, and all the things you should *be* and are not. You think honesty is having your guilt confirmed completely.

We ask you: Do you wish to carry this burden? If the answer is no, there are a few simple steps that you are ready to take. We ask you: What is the biggest "should" that an alcoholic thinks he should be doing?

Answer: He thinks he should stop drinking, but he does not.

The first step for an alcoholic, is to admit he cannot manage what he thinks he should be doing. What he must accept at this time, is that he cannot manage doing what he thinks he should be doing. He must accept that no matter how hard he tries, he cannot force himself to do anything he thinks he should be doing. What *you* must accept about anything you think you should be doing and are not, is that you cannot manage the doing. Do you not see that guilt has been *your* "motivator" to do those things you think you should be doing? In your insane system, you believe that guilt motivates; that if you feel guilty enough, you will be able to manage doing what you think you should be doing. What you fail to see, is that guilt only burdens you and prevents you from doing anything.

Can you accept that you cannot force yourself to do those things you think you should be doing? It is easy to see that an alcoholic cannot force himself to stop drinking. Why is it so hard for you to see that you cannot force yourself to do anything you think you should be doing? An alcoholic cannot manage alcohol, and broadly speaking, you cannot manage doing anything you think you should be doing and are not. That is the first step: To admit you can do nothing about what you think you should be doing. Can you see there is no room for guilt in this? Your guilt came from thinking you had to somehow manage doing all the things you thought you should be doing and were not.

The second step is in seeing your Higher Power is there to look after what you should be doing and guiding you to do it.

The third step is saying simply: "Will You look after all the things I think I should be doing, and make sure I do those things that will be of most service to You."

In Step Four, we make a list of all those things we think we should be doing and are not; all those things we think we should be and are not.

The next few steps are saying to our Higher Power:

> **"Here is the list of all the things I think
> I should be doing and have been unable
> to make myself do. Will You be the judge
> of what I need to do to find Peace and
> to extend it? I accept I cannot do all the
> things I think I should do; but with Your
> help, I will do that which is necessary to
> see and share Peace with others. These
> are the things I wish to do; these are my
> character defects that I think I should be
> releasing. I humbly ask You to remove all
> defects which stand in the way of Peace. I
> humbly ask You to remove those things I
> have been trying to remove. I humbly ask
> You to assist me in doing those things I've
> been trying to do."**
>
> **Amen**

Back To Childhood

Most of us do not like going back and looking into some areas of our childhood. There were times when we felt totally helpless and powerless over certain happenings. We don't like getting in touch with those feelings of shame, anxiety, and fear. We do not like to re-feel those moments. Helplessness is a feeling we avoid most of all. We do not like the insecurity of getting in touch with those old feelings of abandonment and of loneliness; of feeling separate and somehow different. We resist feelings of guilt, feelings of not being strong enough, big enough, or knowing enough.

We carry burdens of shame. We carry burdens of feeling unloved and unwanted. We carry burdens of not feeling as good as those around us. We carry burdens of feeling inferior and somehow deficient. We all have a feeling of loss in some form or another, which is almost unbearable to feel again. Sometimes in our childhood we have felt unable to have a say in what has happened to us; we felt lost, alone, frightened, and totally helpless. These are experiences we have tried to avoid ever feeling or reliving again. We felt out of control then, and we have sought to control ever since in order never to be or feel helpless again.

There are old wounds we do not wish reopened, old memories and situations that we do not wish to face. We are sick with fear and misunderstanding of those experiences that have happened to us. To look again at those things we have shut up so tightly within us, is indeed fearful.

But, we finally realize that all our attempts to shut up what has hurt us, has only kept the hurt buried deep within us.

The experiences, and our conclusions about them, have not been healed — they are festering inside and draining our well-being. They are keeping love and acceptance from us. We have kept our fears and misunderstandings in darkness. We have hidden our shame, our feelings of being unlovable and unwanted, and we have hoped to God that no one would ever see them. We have denied and kept back many feelings just in case feeling anything would bring back the helplessness of those old situations. We have denied feelings of joy, closeness, and happiness, just in case others would see the shame of our fear and helplessness.

There is a child within us, still feeling helpless, still feeling unwanted and unloved, still feeling very frightened, and wanting desperately to reach out. It is for this child that we must go back and write about all we have hidden and sought to forget. It is for this child's release and healing that we must prepare to share with another so our child may see its beauty and innocence. We have controlled so much in order to keep this child safe, and to keep the child within us from ever being hurt again. But to bury our hurt and shame is to keep it. It is time we asked for help to let all the old hurts go.

Going on a journey back to childhood brings us in touch with all our old feelings of helplessness. We are afraid of the journey. But in us is a child still wanting love, still wanting laughter, still wanting to reach out, and still wanting to be accepted for who he or she is. There is a child simply wanting to be. We make an inventory, so this child may laugh and walk in the sunshine again. We make an inventory, so this child may trust and let others in again. We make an inventory, so this child may know how to play and live again. We do not make this journey alone, for in the midst of our feelings of powerlessness and helplessness, there is One Who has all Power and He will walk beside us on our journey. His Light is strong to shine on any darkness we find. His Love is strong to dissolve and replace any fear we see. We do not walk alone. Together with our Higher Power we go to find the child and bring it home.

My Name Is Leanne And I'm A Controloholic

When I try to control the outcome of anything, I lose sight of Peace. I lose sight of the possibility that everything is working out in the best possible way. I become consumed with efforts to have things go my way. I get tense just writing about it. And the ironic thing is that whenever things turn out the way I've tried to control, it still doesn't bring me happiness. I still don't let go of my control. I find myself immediately looking around for what else I can control, or how I can keep control of what I have achieved.

I have a barometer built into my body — my neck. Anytime I want to control something, my neck gets tighter and tighter as a reminder that I must control a particular person or situation. The more I want to control, the more my neck hurts until it has thrown my whole body out of whack. Aspirins don't release my neck, chiropratic adjustments don't help. The only thing that releases my pain is when I finally admit what it is I am trying to control so desperately, and ask for a little willingness to have my goal replaced with God's Will and Peace.

It's amazing how many things I want to control and still more amazing how doggedly I hold onto this control even when I've seen time and time again the tension it brings. I've seen how my controls make situations feel even more stuck. The more I try to insist or control how things should be, the more stuck the situation or relationship becomes. The more I want to control my husband's habit of keeping our back room in chaos, the more chaotic it becomes. The more I want to control my time, the more it seems interfered with. The more I try to control people being on time, the later they become and the angrier I get. The more I try to control my temper, the more I blow up at people. The more I try to control how our home should be organized, the more disorganized it becomes. And on it goes. I even try to control giving up control.

However, in the midst of this chaos and tension is the realization that my controls don't work and before my neck or the situation becomes too crazy, I can ask for God's Sanity instead of my desperate attempts to control. This means, that for me, instead of being in a black depression for months, the fear and desperation need last only minutes or hours. As soon as I realize I am back pushing or controlling a certain outcome, then I realize I have a choice. I can continue to push harder, continuing in my tension and unhappiness, or I can choose to let my goal of control go and have Ease given instead. To be truthful, I still, at times, choose to control even harder, just in case my controls may still work, but all the signs are there that they don't — the tension, the fear, the feeling of being out of control, the confusion, the anger or even rage, the bitterness, the disappointment, the stuckedness, and most of all the desperation of an addict, addicted to control.

I can't stop my addiction, but I have a Higher Power that restores Sanity, when I let Him. Someone once defined insanity as "doing the same thing again and again, hoping that this time it will work". That's me with control. Even though I know it doesn't really bring me what I want, I continue to use it again and again, hoping this time it will be different.

However, I now know that wanting to control is my addiction and with this knowledge I can ask for God's Ease instead of my desperation, wherever I am having problems. And, wherever I am having problems is where I think I know best, where I think I must have "this" to be happy, so I must control to make sure I get it.

To be sure, there are still a few areas in my life that I don't want to stop controlling. These are the "problem" areas in my relationships, my home, my work. But even here, I can ask for willingness to give up my controls. Sanity can come anywhere when I am willing to give up my control to the Higher Power for His solution.

I never saw before that I had a choice. That's the big difference between then and now. Then, I thought that I had to control and was wretchedly unhappy because I couldn't control much of anything that happened to me. I was bitter, cynical, and my life felt continually out of control. It never occurred to me that trying to control with my self-will was the problem. I thought my problem was that I hadn't learned how to control properly yet. I took courses on control, tried harder to control, and drank and took more pills to control.

I was up to a bottle of valium a day, trying to control. I was trying to control my feelings of desperation that my controlling wasn't working. I wanted to die. The only problem I thought I had was that the bottle of valium a day no longer worked — I was out of control in spite of the pills. I could no longer control anything and I was devastated.

*When Maynard solemnly told me that I was a junkie, I was tremendously insulted. I could see **he** had a drinking problem but my only problem was that my pills weren't working as they should. As soon as I discovered another brand of pill, I would be back in control. But I couldn't find anything that would control my feelings and my actions — they came in spite of my attempts to control. I came to Narcotics Anonymous and Alcoholics Anonymous in despair — nothing was working. I could control nothing in my life and this, I thought, was the tragedy. But with the Twelve Step Program, I found out that finally admitting I could control nothing was the good news. It was my release. The problem had been my trying to control everything. It's called self-will. The definition of any addict is really "self-will run riot" — self-will wanting to control. And I indeed was an addict — not only of drugs and booze, but of control itself.*

More and more I realized I was not just addicted to one or two substances, but I was addicted to trying to control my life. And one area after another needed to be given to my Higher Power so Sanity could return.

Yes, daily there are all sorts of things I want and attempt to control. But I've seen control is my addiction. Each time I get carried away, I can admit this and ask for help in going beyond my controloholic will. I have seen another way. The desperation is never as deep, the tension is never as strong, the attempts to control are never as long. The feeling of loneliness lasts only as long as I am trying to control. Life opens up daily and gives gifts far beyond my control.

That's why this Program works — it's beyond my control.

Step Five

"We admitted to God, to ourselves, and to another human being the exact nature of our wrongs."

We come to this realization: Everyone wants to open and reach out to each other, but we all have one very limiting condition — "You go first."

Step Five

We all like to create a good impression. We like others to think well of us. We like attention and we like to feel others' approval. But most of us have never felt we deserved this approval, this acceptance. We didn't *feel* good enough, we didn't feel we had *done* anything good enough; we didn't feel we *were* good enough. We felt that if anyone truly knew us, they would dislike or even despise us. So, we created a person we thought people would like. We put on a mask, we put on a front, and seldom did we acknowledge our true desires, thoughts, or feelings. We became someone else — we were not ourselves — we were not real.

So afraid are we now to be ourselves that the Fifth Step seems very frightening. Many of us, for the first time, are going to let someone see what we are really like. This has been fearful, for we have thought that should anyone see this, they would be repulsed and no longer wish to have anything to do with us. For the first time many of us are going to admit to ourselves just what we have done, and what we have become.

We are afraid of being real, for that never seemed good enough. We are afraid to show many of our feelings, for we have condemned them and judged them harshly. Now, we are requested to share these same thoughts and feelings with another person. We are requested to be honest and hold nothing back.

Most of us are afraid of honesty, for we have played another role for so long. But this role is suffocating us. The mask is stifling our being, and we can no longer breathe. We have to become real, to be who we are and to start wherever we happen to be coming from. We can play our roles no longer, for they are taking life from us. We want to be ourselves and we are afraid — we don't know how. We have pretended to be someone else for so long — we don't know how.

Step Five is our beginning. We are ready to let another person really see us and everything we have used. We are willing to take this risk. We are willing to step from behind the impressions we have been trying to make, so another can see us, and so we can finally be ourselves.

This is a journey to find ourselves. It is not a journey of condemnation; it is a journey that will allow us to be all those things we have been trying so desperately to pretend we were. In sharing our weakness, we will find our strength. In sharing our fears, we will find our courage. In sharing our mistakes, we will find our answers. In sharing our defects, we will find our gifts. In sharing ourselves truly with another, we will find it is okay to *be;* we will find it is our *realness* that those around us wanted all the time. It is *we* they wanted, not the image or impression. In this step, we give up what we thought we had to be, in order to find the freedom of simply being and of simply coming from wherever we happen to be. In this step we find acceptance.

Starting From Where You Are

Starting from where you are is accepting that you are where you need to be, and where you need to look. Acceptance of where you are is Love. For here there is no judgment, just acceptance and faith that what needs to happen will happen. To make a beginning is to admit honestly and truly where you are. By this admittance, are you asking for God to guide your lives. In this sense is beginning or starting where you are, the acceptance of the presence of God.

It is by saying you are where you are, and the realization you cannot go it alone that calls forth the presence of God. *The only question when you do not like where you are coming from is: "Am I admitting where I am, and do I choose to let God release me from my fears and controls?"*

Release is not *your* function — admittance is. You are still trying to do it yourself; for you have not yet realized you are the newcomer each moment. Not only must you take Step One when you first come into the Program, you must take Step One each moment — for each moment is a realization *you* do not have to do it. You wisely look at each newcomer's struggles to do it himself. You regard him with empathy for you know what this feels like. Never are you not the newcomer. Each moment need you realize you must admit you are powerless but your Higher Power is not. When you give up your life to His direction, you also give up your burdens, your worries, and your concerns. This is the only true direction.

Question: What is self-hate?

Answer: Understand, you have no self-hate, but you do
              hate the image you have made. You hate the
              image, for you can never control it absolutely.
              Self-hate is attempting to run your life according
              to **your** will. You will never succeed and will hate
              that self that prevents you from doing so. Letting
              God guide you, there will be no room for a self of
              your making.

*As I was watching a ventriloquist and his dummy,
I recognized that my dummy self was the role I was
playing, was an act, was only my personality. The
puppeteer part of me was a controloholic hiding
behind his dummy act. The more I refined my act, the
more lonely I felt, because others either praised or
rejected the dummy act, leaving me in an isolation of
my own making. In Step Five, coming out from behind
the masks of my personality and taking a chance,
even on being rejected, was the release for my
chronic loneliness.*

— Maynard

A Show Of Strength

What you need to realize is that defense of any kind is to hide a belief in weakness.

You have gone to great efforts to prove your strength, to prove you can confront anything, to prove you would not back down or run away. But what you have not seen is that these proofs were only necessary, because they hid a belief in weakness.

You have been hiding a belief in weakness, which comes from making your own decisions and attempting to manage your direction. By yourself, you are weak — it as simple as that. *Everything* you have called strength has been to hide weakness. The greatest "act of bravery" you will ever perform is to forgive.

What we wish to emphasize to you now is the real strength that comes from forgiveness. Your strength lies here. Forgiveness is strength, because it would join you with others and with your Source. All *your* strengths have been cultivated to hide your weaknesses.

Admit your weakness now, not out of shame but out of relief that you are not called upon to be strong by yourself. Yes, by yourself you are weak and have been hiding this with your creations of strength. Hide weakness no longer but admit and ask for the strength of forgiveness to join you with all things. Celebrate! Come out of your hiding into the Light.

I Don't Know How

This admittance is the one you fear the most. You hide not knowing how with a desperate dread. The last thing that you want anyone to know is that you don't know how. You will practice avoidance, you will surround the area with confusion and commotion — anything rather than admit that you don't know how.

And there are so many areas that you know nothing about. You don't know how to open, how to be nice, how to be a conversationalist, how to be a good lover, how to be the hostess with the mostest, how to feel, how to share, how to let go, how to take Step Five and so on.

In anguish you cover these areas with pretending, fakery — anything that will distract anyone from knowing that you don't know how.

You have never stopped to question one small detail — who decided that you had to know how? Who decided that you had to know how to feel, how to get along, how to open...? Who took this responsibility and put it on your shoulders? When did God ever tell you that you had to know how?

We say to you: The entire goal of this Program is to bring you to one realization: *Not only do you not have to know how, by yourself it is impossible to know how. Your knowing how has been the separation. Your biggest admittance is: I DO NOT KNOW HOW.*

When you can truly make this admittance, there will be a relief as you have never felt before. Understand, your knowing how is not necessary, your willingness to be shown how is.

Any time you wish to hide, be assured somewhere you have decided: "I should know how but I don't, and I hope to hell that no one finds out."

Child of God, of course you do not know how, for you were meant to be with God where there is All Knowing. Come to the Father by saying: "I do not know how. You do. Please show me."

This is not a moment of anguish, but of gratitude, for the responsibility was never yours.

Patterns

We, as controloholics, have found ourselves in the same situations of conflict over and over again. These situations of conflict we call patterns. By ourselves, we do not always see or recognize our patterns. But when we share our situations of conflict with another, he or she will assist us in seeing the crazy patterns that have dominated our lives. We find we are too close to the patterns — being in a pattern does not allow us to step outside and observe it impartially.

We find that as a result of trying to control our lives, that we are caught up in many strange patterns. When we write down or do an inventory of our lives, we will catch a glimpse of recurring patterns that have been like threads throughout our past. We finally share in order to see our patterns of destruction, our patterns of self-hate, our patterns of revenge and sabotage, our patterns in choosing inappropriate partners, our patterns of lack and denial, our patterns of keeping out love and support. Whatever our pattern has been, by ourselves we are too close to see it objectively.

We share with another, and with God, every aspect of our lives that has not been resolved, that has not been healed. What we have denied has been too much for us — by ourselves we cannot see. We let others see our lives, so they may assist us in seeing those patterns that have kept healing from us. We begin to see, with the help of another, just what conclusions we have made that have been erroneous or harmful to us. With the help of another, we are able to see our patterns clearly. With the help of another, we are able to look at the guilt we carry, at our patterns of denial and destruction. We are finally open to the help of another in truly looking at our lives and in honestly seeing those patterns for the first time. With our patterns in the open, we now have a choice — we can keep them, or we can call upon the assistance of our Higher Power to release them. Our patterns have imprisoned us, but with the help of another, we can be set free.

Waking Up

Any time a pattern is revealed, it will seem as if that is all you see. It will seem as if many things are surfacing that were not there before. We wish to point out what is happening. Any time the pattern is revealed, you simply become aware of all the areas in which you use it. In other words, you begin to wake up to the pattern in order to release it. Once it is seen in *all* its aspects, it will not hold the same power for you and will finally be seen through.

Coming Clean

There is something about coming clean with another that cleanses us. We share, because this prevents us from hiding any longer. Any illusion we might carry about our ability to hide is dispelled, when we begin to share with another.

Coming clean is so important in our recovery. We do not drag up the past in order to condemn ourselves; we bring it up in order to let it go. Our story must be told initially for our own sanity and eventually for the sanity of others. In our Higher Power's hands the sharing of our story becomes a useful thing.

We have hidden our feelings, our thoughts, our hurts and our actions for so long that we are afraid to have another see what is in us. But for our own sanity, we must come clean. What we would hide and protect another from seeing is what keeps us from seeing the gift that we really are. It keeps us from seeing our own value and it keeps us from receiving all the love and support that is given to us.

We tell God and we tell another human being the exact nature of what we have done or failed to do. We hold back nothing, for in our recovery we must come clean.

We will have two surprises in store for us with our admittance. The first surprise comes when we realize that the one we share with will not be repulsed or offended with our sharing. They will only be concerned that we bring all our darkness for release. There is nothing that we have done that cannot be forgiven. It is not what we have done that has offended others — it is our insistence on hiding our actions and intents; it is our denial of what we have done and the excuses we have made in the doing that has kept others from us.

For our recovery and our sanity, we can be closed no longer. We can deny nothing. We no longer make excuses or justifications — we come clean. Our fear of sharing is great, but our fear of loneliness and insanity is greater, and beyond our fear is a desire for healing, for forgiveness, and for release.

Our second surprise comes when we realize that the sharing of our story may be of some value to another. The story itself has no value — our *willingness to come clean* with our story is priceless. We share our story with others in order to keep coming clean and in order to share the gift of healing so others, too, may come from behind their hiding place.

In our hands, our story has been one of pain and anguish. In God's hands, the sharing of our story may be a gift to others, who like us, have never had the courage to come into the open with one another.

My Name Is Maynard And I'm A Controloholic

I still can't see any value in just sharing me. I still have a desire to select some impressive events from my past, some impressive plans about the future, some impressive people I could name drop, or some fantastic theories to talk about. To honestly share where I am coming from, at this time, just simply does not compute.

When my sponsor asks me to share my being, that he wants my story and not my explanations or theories, this still does not compute. My mind draws a blank.

As far back as I can remember, just being me or being just me was never good enough. I always felt I had to do or accomplish something extraordinary, to be with someone important or special, to put on an act of my best behavior or strive at least to be better than I was. With all this striving, I still felt like a second-class citizen on the outside looking in. Most of my life I was convinced that I was feeling like this, because during the Second World War, at the age of eight, I was actually relocated from my native Latvia to Germany and later at the age of fifteen, displaced from Germany to Canada. I was convinced that being the new kid on the block and just learning a new language and customs, was the cause for my always feeling like the outsider.

Soon I discovered that alcohol could make me feel equal to others and at times more equal than others. Even in equality, like in other areas in my life, I either felt less equal or more equal than others. If equality had been a drink, I would have ordered a double — I could never get enough of it.

So I strived to be better than equal, more than equal, sought to impress, to put on an act to cover up my not feeling enough. I think they call it an ego trip now-a-days. In short, I lost sight of who I was and even today, on my own, without God's help, I cannot manage just to be me, manage to be satisfied just to be me, no matter how deeply I desire just to be me. Even when no one is impressed, I am still addicted to impressing.

Today, I have a deep desire to come clean, to be me without really knowing how to accomplish this. At this point in time I am willing to admit what I have been "using" to have things work my way. I have used commotions and obsessive behaviors to detract from my inability to make things work. I have used my addictions that have tainted and permeated all areas of my life. I have used justification, rationalization, denial, blame, and many other controloholic symptoms.

My life had become a clever facade of clever acts. My head seemed to be working overtime in high gear at all times and my heart seemed choked off and isolated.

At this time, sharing where I am is still difficult. It feels like doing an open heart surgery on myself. A lobotomy might be easier, for it would cover more familiar ground.

*I still have a tendency to seek for my solutions outside of myself. I am still a controloholic, you know. No one can give me solutions that I want to have my way, because wanting to have solutions my way is the root cause of all my problems — of anybody's problems. This does not mean that there are no solutions to the problems I perceive, but they are not **my** solutions. This is where I need you, you other self-admitted controloholics, and God.*

*I have the freedom to seek with my solutions all I wish, be it another day, year, or decade. I already know that seeking with and for solutions **my way**, for the problems I perceive, will never bring me lasting healing. I may as well admit again and again that wanting solutions my way is the root cause of my problems. After all, I am a controloholic when I choose to be separate from my Higher Power.*

Step Six

"We were entirely ready to have God remove all defects of character."

Us: *God, do I have to make myself worthy of You?*
God: *No.*

Us: *God, what must I do to prepare myself for You?*
God: *Nothing.*

Us: *God, how may I best help You to remove my defects of character?*
God: *Are you willing?*

Us: *Yes.*
God: *That is enough.*

Step 6

There is a great relief in finally letting the world see us as we truly are. We need no longer carry the burden of guilt for what we have done or for what we have used. We have let another see our resentments, our mistakes, the revenge in our hearts and the little hurt child beyond all these things.

We have shared with another our weaknesses, our defects of character that we have sought so long to hide. We have shared what has kept us in bondage through bitterness and resentment. And having shared, we are finally ready to let these things go. We no longer wish anger and hatred in our lives. We no longer wish the pain of blame and jealousy in our lives. We no longer wish to reject or be rejected. We no longer wish to hurt or be hurt. We no longer wish our grievances. We no longer wish the use of our controls, of our management.

We are finally ready to say: "Enough! I don't want a life like this anymore. I don't want to feel like this anymore. I don't want to carry this garbage anymore. I am ready for everything that has hurt me to be removed from my life. I am ready to let the past go. I am ready for anything that has been defective in my thinking to be replaced with God's gentle vision. I don't want to use my controls any longer." It is this we are ready — entirely ready — to have God remove.

Before, anytime we looked at our difficulties, we were afraid to admit our use of controls, for we thought that if we truly saw what we were doing, we would have to do something about it. We would have to assume guilt and responsibility for all we had done in our lives. We would have to stop the destruction in our lives. Thinking we had to know how to change our lives or how to fix our difficulties was always a big stumbling block. We did not know what to do to change our lives, and we were afraid to start, for we thought that the responsibility for that change would rest squarely on our shoulders.

Step Six takes the responsibility for the change in our lives out of our hands and puts it into the hands of our Higher Power. Our willingness to let go of these defects is needed — that is all — our willingness to give everything we have made — all our mistakes, all our illusions, all our judgments, over to our Higher Power so He can remove them.

This step is radically different from all our previous attempts to change our lives. This step gives all our resentments, fears, and misperceptions to God for His removal. At last we are entirely ready to let God remove what we had always been unable to let go of.

Who Is Willing?

Who is willing to give up what he believes to be true? The most we can ask is that you be willing to *question* what you believe is true. This we are asking. In taking Step Six, you are admitting that what you have thought was true has only made your life unmanageable. Only then are you ready for Step Seven. Do you see the power of admittance?

Ready Or Not

We still like to do things by ourselves. In Step Six, there is a tendency to *make* ourselves ready. We like to help God out. We still think there is something to prepare for. We find it difficult to comprehend that all God needs is our *willingness* to let Him remove whatever is in the way of our healing. Readiness in this step is the same as saying, "We were entirely *willing* to have God remove all these defects of character." We are entirely ready when we finally see we have been unable to remove any of the blocks to our well-being — indeed the problem has been our desperate attempts to change our lives by ourselves. There is nothing to prepare. There is nothing to do — except ask. In the acceptance of this, are we entirely ready for our Higher Power's healing to take place.

Where Are You Coming From?

When you approach your Higher Power:

Are you here to ask, or are you here to demand?

Are you here to prove, or are you here to be open to?

Are you here to be right, or are you here to be shown?

Are you asking to have *your* way, or are you asking for *The Way?*

Are you ready to have your life healed, or are you still holding on to your conditions?

There is a polite question we ask each other: "Where do you come from?" Geographically speaking it does not matter, but spiritually speaking it means everything. We have revised the question somewhat to say: "Where are you coming from?" The purpose is two-fold: the first is that by admittance of where we are coming from, we can ask our Higher Power to take us beyond wherever we are; the second purpose is to show that where we come from in our being and asking, will determine the healing and the answer we will hear. If we approach our Higher Power demanding His assistance, then we have approached Him with a closed fist. If we approach with proving or wanting to be right, then we have approached God with a pre-judged or prejudiced conclusion. In essence, then, we are not looking for a solution. Nothing can be removed without our willingness or readiness to have it removed.

If we are asking for explanations for the insanities of our world, they cannot be answered for they are insane; but if we are asking for Sanity in the midst of our world, then the Peace of God can enter.

In taking Step Six, where do you come from — an open hand, or a closed fist? Your willingness to start from where you are, even if it is with a closed fist, will bring healing. Your willingness to come open-mindedly and honestly will bring many answers. Where are you coming from? What is your focus? This will indeed be the difference between hearing and silence; between keeping your blocks or having them removed.

Are You Ready For A Change?

Excerpted from ASKCEPTANCE ©1988 Maynard and Leanne Dalderis Published by Vitagenics Institute Foundation

> *"Please change **all** my perceptions so I may see the innocence of All There Is."*
>
> *Anything that can be seen with forgiveness is change. This is the* only *change there is.*
>
> *Revenge being changed to forgiveness is the only change possible. All else is ego.*
>
> *Anything that **you** think has been changed and it still causes you pain, realize — nothing has been changed.*
>
> *Nothing is changed until you are willing to be shown forgiveness in each situation.*
>
> *Resistance to this change "hurts". The change of seeing things through forgiveness does **not** hurt.*
>
> *You can only change a perception of a situation by seeing it with forgiveness instead of judgment.*
>
> *Are you willing for the change of forgiveness in all areas of your life?*
>
> *Are you ready for a change of heart? Are you willing to see from a heart of forgiveness?*

Forgiveness is the only change that will heal.

To see everything, including yourself, with total forgiveness, is the only change possible.

*All **you** need is a little willingness to have your mind changed to a forgiving mind.*

*Only your Higher Power can change your mind. Only **you** can ask Him to do so.*

Any change is an opportunity to see Peace; and Forgiveness is the only change there is.

Nothing that has not been given to your Higher Power can change.

"Higher Power, I give You my mind for You to change to a forgiving mind."

"You can change my mind."

"Higher Power, You are responsible for changing my mind. I am responsible for the willingness to let You."

How your mind is going to be changed is not up to you.

Are you willing to have your mind changed to see the situation already healed?

"I am not in charge of any change of mind, God is."

Any hurt to any change, is your resistance to that change.

"Only You can change my mind here."

The special relationship, or the relationship we try to control, never changes — the forms may change, but nothing really changes.

In a Holy Relationship, or a relationship that our Higher Power is in charge of — everything changes for our healing.

Step Seven

"We humbly asked God to remove our shortcomings."

*The Spirit of Humility heals
all our humiliations.*

Step Seven

It seems too easy. All we have to do is ask God to remove our shortcomings? This seems too simple. We, who are used to the complications and manipulations of a controloholic mind, have difficulty grasping this simple solution. "That's all there is to it?" Yes, that is all there is to having our shortcomings removed.

This step is difficult for a complex mind to understand. But the Truth *is* simple. Having God manage our lives and remove what does not work is what will keep our lives simple and free from the anguish we have experienced up until now.

We have been unable to control our lives even though we have used everything in an attempt to do so. We are not required to remove anything. We are only requested to ask that God do it for us. This is humility. We humbly ask, because we finally realize we are unable to remove what has brought so much pain in our relationships with the rest of the world. We are finally going to ask God unreservedly for His assistance. Humility simply says: "I can't. Will You please help me?"

We ask humbly for God's assistance to remind us that it is not up to us to direct this assistance. We place the removal in God's hands, to be removed in His time. We no longer direct the how, when, where or why; we no longer demand. In humbly asking, we place all these things in His care.

Yes, it is a simple step, but it is the only solution which will work in our recovery from a controloholic life. We come humbly, because our efforts have brought no results. Our efforts have only led to addictions. This is a simple step, and because of its simplicity, because God is managing the removal — we will find it works.

Stop It!

You have begun to notice how many areas of your life you have been trying to control. You have also begun to see that your trying to control is really the difficulty to all the problems that you are experiencing.

You wish to go beyond all this. It is time to give up the managing and get on with things, or rather, let things be got on with. So you resolve: "I will stop trying to control in all these areas!" You determine that as trying to control is the problem, you will simply stop doing it. And so you begin to stop it. You try to stop managing control of your business, your finances, your health, your relationships, and in your efforts you try to stop others from managing their lives. You try to stop everything.

Lately you wonder why you feel on hold, stuck, held back. What is the problem? The problem is simply this: "I can't go forward until I stop managing, until I stop trying to control, for I have seen that trying to control stops me from going forward. Therefore, until I manage to stop managing, I can't go forward."

Let us gently point out something to you: *YOU ARE NOT REQUIRED TO STOP ANYTHING.* This is resistance. You are only asked to admit your management, your controls, when you observe yourself doing so. Once this is admitted, you are not required to stop it. You are only asked for the willingness to have your Higher Power manage the situation. Do you not see that trying to stop anything is back into trying to control? The truth is — you cannot manage to stop anything by yourself. Yes, you may appear to stop in one area of management; but if you are doing the managing, there will still be a state of dis-ease.

With your Higher Power, simply admitting your controls and asking for His direction will bring about a state of Ease in which, not only is your management stopped — it is released.

Have you not seen an alcoholic who has decided he will stop drinking by himself? He may do so, yet the state of dis-ease or management continues to be present. You can feel the tension with which he is stopping himself.

The goal is not to stop; it is to see that beyond all our attempts to control is a way of Peace — a way of Ease.

You are not required to stop or remove anything, for truly, by yourself you cannot even stop this. But you are asked to be willing to be gently led beyond your controls to the way of Ease.

Humbly Asked...

We humbly ask. We are not required to be humiliated before we ask. There is a vast difference between humility and humiliation.

With humiliation there is guilt; with humility there is release.

With humiliation you must change or correct yourself; with humility there is acceptance of self.

Humiliation would take our strength from us. Humility lets us see the strength in our Higher Power.

Humiliation says, "I should have known better." Humility asks for God's knowing.

Humiliation never gets over what is perceived as done to us. Humility forgives.

Humiliation is to bring down. Humility is to let be.

Humiliation is to seek attention. Humility is to listen.

Humiliation is insistence. Humility is opening to assistance.

Humiliation is telling or demanding. Humility is asking.

Humiliation only sees guilt. Humility is seeing the innocence.

Humiliation is holding on to our way. Humility is getting out of the way.

Humiliation is trying to be enough. Humility is seeing our completeness.

Humiliation is in *our* time. Humility is in *God's* time.

Humiliation is deciding what we need. Humility is letting God decide what we need.

Humiliation is hiding our fears. Humility is admitting them.

Humiliation is wanting to be special. Humility is seeing our connection with others.

Humiliation is thinking we have to make it. Humility is realizing we have it given.

Humiliation would hold on to. Humility would let go of.

Humiliation would curse the darkness. Humility would make light of it.

Humiliation would go it alone. Humility would ask for our Higher Power's guidance.

Humiliation would dwell in mistakes. Humility would admit them for our Higher Power's correction.

Humiliation is trying to do it ourselves. Humility is letting God lead us.

Humiliation is what we demand of ourselves. Humility is what God asks of us.

Humiliation is a life run on self-will. Humility is a life given to our Higher Power.

A Bedtime Story

Beyond all my controls and attempts to manage my life, there is a child who just wants to be loved and accepted. The child inside of me is very insecure and very frightened of showing itself and letting people see her. I've been very unkind to my child, judging her behavior, her thoughts and her feelings as unlovable, and trying to change her so that people and God will love her and accept her. It's hard for me to understand that I don't have to somehow change or be different for a Higher Power to help me or for my Higher Power to love me. I don't have to make myself more lovable or acceptable — I'm loved already.

This story is for the child in all of us who just wants to come home.

— Leanne

Once upon a time, there was a little child standing on a doorstep. It was very cold outside. Night was coming and the wind started to rise. Inside the house, it was nice and warm and it was filled with a magnificent light. The child could see through the window that, indeed, the home was warm and filled with love. Although the child could not see it, he could feel a presence inside the home. The presence was warm and radiated a tremendous love. This presence gently invited the child into the home where he would be made welcome and warm in that wondrous light.

The child heard the voice calling him home and he began to cry. He cried because he had not yet learned how to tie his shoes and did not think he would be admitted into the home until he had learned this task. Indeed, the shoes themselves were on the wrong feet. To make matters even worse, the child was wearing thick and heavy mittens, which made it impossible to either tie his shoes by himself, or reach up to open the door that led to the warmth and comfort inside.

Through his tears and sobs of anguish, the child heard the voice calling to him again:

"It's okay," said the voice, "You don't have to know how to tie your shoes before you can come inside. Come inside and I will teach you."

But the child only cried louder and again tried unsuccessfully to tie his shoes before he could come home.

Still, the voice lovingly encouraged him to come home anyway with his shoes untied and offered again to teach him.

"But my shoes are on the wrong feet, and I don't know how to put them on properly," the child wailed.

The voice gently answered: "Don't worry about it, it does not matter, come into my home and I will teach you this too. Come in where it is warm and let me help you to put your shoes on the right feet."

But the child, growing more and more cold, sadly shook its head. "I can't open the door, my mittens are too clumsy and they keep sliding off the handle."

"Fear not," the voice gently said, "For I will open the door for you. I will make sure the door is always open for you. I will never let the door to my home close upon you. You do not have to know how to open it. Just ask me and I will remind you that my door is always open. Please come in out of the cold."

In utmost desperation and embarrassment, the child cried, "But now you really won't want me in your home, because I was scared and wet my pants. I can't come into your home like this!"

And the voice, even more gently and more lovingly replied: "It does not matter. I only want you to come home. I do not see what is soiled, I only want my child home."

Still the child hesitated and whimpered softly: "I don't know how to come in. I am so cold now I don't know if I can walk into your home. I hurt all over and I'm scared. My shoelaces are still untied. My shoes are still on the wrong feet, my pants are wet, and I can do nothing with my hands so clumsy and awkward. I don't know how to come home," the child sobbed.

And as always, the child heard the voice even more loving and even more encouraging: "Do not be afraid. Ask and wherever you are I will find you. I will carry you home and with your willingness lead you across the threshold into the warmth of my care. If you have no willingness, ask and I will give you mine. You need do nothing to come home. Simply ask and my door is open. You don't have to accomplish or know how to do anything, for I will teach you whatever it is you need to know. You do not have to correct your wrongs before you can come home. You do not have to be clean. For when you are home, I will assist you in any way to leave all pain and misperceptions behind. You do not have to be well to come into my home, for healing occurs in my home, not outside of it. You do not have to get rid of all your twisted beliefs and anger to come home, for when you are at home, I will help you reinterpret everything that has been fearful, and replace it with my love."

The child had grown very cold and weary indeed during his struggle on the doorstep. His shoelaces were still untied. His shoes were still on the wrong feet. His pants were frozen. His hands, encased in his mittens, had become numb trying to open the door. He could no longer move them. He could no longer do anything by himself. He only wanted to come home. And in the midst of his numbness and fear, he remembered one thing — he remembered to ask. He asked for the presence to help him across the threshold into the warmth of the home. And in that moment he was home — home with all the warmth, all the light, and all the love.

The end or Maybe the beginning...

A Waking Up Story

You are the child on the doorstep. You, too, have many
conditions before you can come home. Before you can ask
for God's knowledge, you think you must figure out how
everything works. Before you can ask for healing, you think
you must prepare yourself with the right tools, methods, and
affirmations. Before you can ask for God's assistance, you
think you must first accomplish certain things by yourself.
Before you can ask for God's love and forgiveness, you think
you must get rid of all your resentments and all your unloving
thoughts. Before you can accept God's gifts, you think you
must make yourself worthy through sacrifice, denial and pain.
Before you can receive God's blessing, you think you must
make yourself pure. Before you can receive God's honesty, you
think you must get rid of all your dishonesty and deceit. And
before you let in God's Love, you think you must learn to love
yourself and others.

And like the child, you stand on the doorstep of God's Love,
with all your conditions, growing colder and colder, attempting
to do all these things before you can come home. You even
think you must know the way home before you can ask
for direction.

But you, like the child, are only asked to see that you can
come home. You can ask God to enter even if you have done
none of the things you think you should have. You do not have
to make yourself innocent to ask for God's Innocence.

You do not have to prepare yourself for healing. What
if healing could come whether you had done the right
preparations or not? What if healing could come whether you

were deserving or not? What if healing could come, even if your thoughts were still twisted and unforgiving, even if you still controlled and tried to manage your life? What if healing could come, even if you haven't managed to be honest and truthful? What if healing could come, whether you said the right prayers or not? What if healing could come, even if you did not know how to let God in? What if healing could come, simply because you have asked God to come beyond all your anger, all your methods, all your controls, all your resistance, to bring you home?

What if you, too, just like the child, could ask God to lead you home, even if you had accomplished nothing towards finding a way home?

You see, the irony of all your conditions is this: However you think you need to prepare yourself to come home, you will not be able to do so, for it is only with God that our conditions can be healed, that we can find our way home. It is only with God that we can be given Knowing, that we can be given forgiveness, that we can find direction, that we can discover honesty, that we can find vision, that our misperceptions can be corrected. It is only with God that we can be shown another way.

We are asked to come home now. There is nothing to prepare — for God will give us Knowing and God will use whatever we give Him for our healing. Like a child, we ask for God to lead us and in this we are prepared for what is needed. We do not have to know how to do anything; we do not have to get rid of anything to ask for God to come into our lives, for it is finally the willingness to let Him in, whether our conditions are fulfilled or not, that will bring us home.

Step Eight

"We made a list of all persons we had harmed, and became willing to make amends to them all."

In making our amends we do not mend fences, we become willing to have them taken down.

Step Eight

Guilt is a heavy burden to bear. We, who have sought to control our lives, carry guilt for many things. And now, to relieve ourselves of this burden, we make a list of all those we have harmed; and we become willing to see the slate wiped clean. We become willing to admit, to be totally honest about those in our lives that we had acted less than loving towards.

The word "harmed" makes us feel guilty right away, for we ourselves are very afraid to hurt or be hurt. Some of us believe we have caused nothing but harm, while others of us pretend that our actions, that our controls, have had no effect at all on those around us.

We make a list of those we had harmed, not so we may see the "irreparable" damage we may have done, but so we may examine our own intent. What was our intent towards these people? Was it not usually to control? To manage? To manipulate?

On our list we place those people we have ignored, those people we have slighted, those people we have deliberately sought to hurt or cause harm to. We write down those people we have been closed or unforgiving towards. We write down those we have been too busy for; those we have had no time for. We write down those people we have judged and condemned. We write down those we had taken from and have not replaced our taking. We write down those that have not received our best performance in what they have hired us to do. We write down those we had lied to; those we have cheated or shortchanged in one way or another. We write down those we have actively offended; those who have felt the brunt of our anger and rage; those who have felt our abuse. We write down those we have pretended with; those we have not been open or honest with. We write down, in essence, all those relationships where our intent has not been loving. And at the very top of this list, we must not forget to place ourselves, for who have we harmed the most but ourselves.

The source of the guilt we carry lies in our intent. We have intended to take rather than to give, to hurt rather than to give healing, to blame rather than to forgive, to judge rather than to accept, to offer closedness rather than opening, to offer dishonesty rather than total honesty.

Our intent now is to become willing to make amends to all those with whom our intentions had come from our desire to control, to have things our way. For us to be free from guilt, finally free from this burden, our intention must be much different now — our intention is to make amends.

We may not be able to "make up" for our previous actions, but we can become willing for total honesty to come into our lives. We can finally be honest with these people, and what we are honest about is what our intentions have been towards them, and our willingness to have these intentions amended, to have these intentions changed, to have these intentions healed. Our intent now is to have all our relationships with those we have sought to control — healed.

The burden of guilt, as we honestly look at our previous intentions, appears overwhelming. Most of our actions have come from closedness and control. But we are not asked to make our amends alone. With some people we might not even be willing to make amends; we may still want revenge rather than forgiveness; we may still wish to be right. But we wish a clean slate, and for this willingness we may ask our Higher Power. We wish a new beginning. And to have this, there must be nothing left on our slate.

The purpose of this step is not to find ourselves guilty — it is to *release* the guilt we have carried from a life based on controls. Willingness is all that is required with this step. How the amends are to be accomplished is not up to us. We are getting our homes in order; we are cleaning house. And with this willingness, we will be cleansed of the guilt we carry.

> *For me to write things down, has been a serious problem since Grade One. I have avoided jobs that needed writing reports, and I have avoided writing a Step Eight list for over 30 years. I have used every control device to procrastinate, to put off committing this list on paper. Finally, with the help of my Higher Power, having done this step in writing, I see that writing something down makes avoidance more difficult. Writing down makes our Program come alive — this is a living Program. Yes, my talk was cheap, and my excuses for not doing this step in writing were only part of my controloholic dis-ease condition.*
> — *Maynard*

Where Have All The Flowers Gone?

Until our sponsor asked us to admit all the ways we were putting each other down, I didn't realize the extent of my controloholic condition; the extent I was using put-downs, especially with those I loved. In my arrogance I had rationalized these put-downs to be some sort of educational aids, generously bestowed by me to benefit others. I reasoned that the noble ends surely justified my means. My feeling miserable and stuck was deemed to be the required sacrifice to fix our lot.

A tiny willingness to ask God to remove our put-downs, and show us what was there to be grateful for in each other, changed the focus from a "stale-mate" to a loving mate.

— Maynard

You wonder where the tenderness in your relationship went to. You wonder: "Where is the closeness? Where is the affection? Where are those little moments of connectedness?" You shake your head sadly and wonder where it all went. Where is the love? It seems the way of all relationships — they lose the warmth and feeling of being together. Why does the other person have to change so? Why are there so many disagreements, conflicts, and confrontations?

To answer these questions, let us look at the purpose of your encounters together. What are you communicating? How do you speak to each other? What is the purpose of your time together? We say this: Anytime your purpose is to control, you will find yourselves "putting each other down". We ask you this: How many times do you put each other down? You do not realize how much of your time and energy is involved in putting others down. Any time others do not do things your way, you'll put them down.

Let us look at all the ways you put each other down. You put down the way someone in your life dresses, speaks, listens, eats, thinks, laughs, works, organizes, sleeps, socializes. You put down their ideas, jokes, plans, cooking, way of communicating with God, lifestyle, code of ethics, financial awareness, business contacts, ways of celebrating, family, work... and so on.

You do not realize the amount of time spent in this activity. We ask you this question: How much time is spent in "building those in your life up"? This seems like a very strange question. "Why would I want to build someone up?" The point is — you spend so much time tearing your loved ones down, why would you not wish to also consider the support that you could give them?

It is most difficult to control people, when you are building them up. All the things you would wish changed about them would be lost, you think, if you were actually to give support and acceptance to them. But we say: Would it not make more sense to any relationship to be willing to give support to it, rather than to undermine it?

You think you can control a situation by putting someone down. You think you can change others by putting them down.

But what you do not see is that by undermining another, you lose sight of any support or connectedness that is there.

You ask us: *"Where is the closeness?"*

We say: *"How can you see it when you put the other down?"*

You say: *"Why is the other not open to me?"*

We say: *"In what areas have you judged or put the other down?"*

You think putting down is a natural way of communicating. We say: It makes as much sense as sawing off the very branch you are sitting on. What if another was not to be put in his place, but what if the other was to be supported in Who he was? What if your purpose was not to put down, but your purpose was to build up? What a tremendous connection that would be.

Actually your purpose is neither to put down nor to build up. It is to ask to see, with the eyes of gratitude, just what people have to offer and just what you have to offer in support of them. It is not to put down your relationships; it is to give them up — for God to show you all their gifts. It is to watch the growth of Who someone else is and Who you are. Why would you wish to put this down?

Amending Your Ways

We have sought to be right about many things. In our attempts to control our lives and the lives of others, we have had to be right about nearly everything. We have defended our rights, and we have had to step on many toes to do so. So desperate have we been to be right that we have closed off to many people. So desperate have we been to be in control that, at times, we have not cared who we have manipulated or how we have used them.

Our desire to be right has been a mighty addiction. It has consumed everything. We have been very defensive and unapproachable in defending our rights. We have left many broken relationships in a trail behind us, because we would rather be right than see healing in the relationship. We have been right rather than happy, and we have put our rightness ahead of anyone else's happiness. We were right, and we didn't care about the consequences to anyone else. When we wanted to control, we lost sight of how others' lives were affected in the process. We either ignored, forgot about, or pretended that our path of "rightness" affected no one. "That's their problem. I have to do what's right for me."

So, we have been right. In our attempts to control we have proven ourselves right about many things. We were right — people took advantage of us. We were right — no one was there for us.

We were right — that was the way it had to be done. We were right — we had to do it alone. We were right — no one really loved us. We were right — only our controls would work. We were right — to get what we wanted, other people's feelings didn't matter. We were right — being right is what counted. In the midst of all this rightness — were we happy? Did it feel right? Or did something feel very wrong?

It is time to admit where we have been wrong. Understand — anywhere where there is closedness, where a relationship is not healed — we have been wrong. It is time to admit where we have been closed, where we have been trying to be right, where we have been trying to control, where we have been harsh and judgmental, where we have been concerned only about ourselves, where we have placed our being right above both our happiness and others' happiness.

Understand, if we feel resentment or pain in any relationship then it is time to consider — "Perhaps I have been wrong. I no longer wish to be right in this relationship anymore."

It is time to make amends. This is the same as saying it is time to ask for healing. Amends begin when we are ready to consider that we do not have to be right here any more. Our being right no longer comes first. Our willingness to forgive and be forgiven becomes our intent. No longer are we intent on being right.

We have had good intentions, but the intentions have been to be right. We are asked to give up our "good" intentions in order to make amends.

We make a list of all those we have been "right" about for where *we* are right another is wronged. It is time to have our wrongs corrected, to make amends, to be willing to let healing occur.

"If there is pain in any of my relationships, then I am willing to see and admit where I have been wrong, and through my admittance I am willing to see all my relationships amended, all my relationships healed." Step Eight is not a "comfortable" step, for we are now looking at relationships in our lives where we have never wanted a close scrutiny. We have preferred to hide or justify our actions.

We have not wished them to be brought to light. But the very bringing to light of all these dark corners will be our release. All we need do is make a list of all those where there is any discomfort or avoidance. We want wellness and we want to come out of the shadows to walk in all honesty and acceptance. We ask for God's courage to do this step and the step that follows.

Step Nine

"We made direct amends to such people wherever possible, except when to do so would injure them or others."

In our addictions we have been asking for a "fix" — now we ask for God to fix what we have torn apart. This is truly the fix we have been seeking.

Step Nine

We have not been too honest with those in our lives. In fact, in most cases we have not been honest at all. We have been "right", but we are only convinced we are right when we have not been honest. We have been right rather than honest.

We have defended our dishonesty, our rightness, very strenuously, but the truth is — we have not been very honest.

For our peace of mind, it is time to come clean. This disturbs us, for the waters of our relationships are muddy with our dishonesty. The greatest amendment to make is to become honest with others. We have not been open or honest with those in our lives — we have pretended, we have white-washed, we have covered up, but we have not let them see the tricks of our manipulation or our desperate attempt to be right in the relationship. When we were trying to control, we have used our relationships for our own narrow purposes, and in our use of them we have abused them.

What we use to control becomes abuse. It is time to be honest about what we have used our relationships for. This is most embarrassing, for in all cases where we have sought to control, our use of relationships has been most selfish. To actually admit this to the one we have been using is quite humbling.

We allow others to see beyond our pretense and to see the reality of our controloholic addiction. We see that the greatest amend we can make is to be totally honest with whomever we have had intentions of controlling. The greatest harm we have done has been our refusal to be open and honest with others.

By now we have sought to fool others and ourselves for so long that honesty does not come easily. We are not sure we are not just fooling ourselves again. In this, too, we need help for honesty. *Our* honesty has become an atrophied function. At this time we may ask for God's Honesty, for God's amendments.

In some cases, the sharing of our honesty is not appropriate, but the admittance of our intent to ourselves in these cases is crucial. For once we consider *others'* feelings and what is best in *their* lives. We go through the process with each person regardless of whether we physically make the amend or not. It is time we saw our intentions and had our intentions amended. It is time we admitted our dishonesty and chose honesty instead.

We ask God to guide our amends. We ask Him to choose the most appropriate time and place to make these amends. And we ask Him to look after how another will receive our amends. It is not up to us to anticipate how another should react to our amends. We are willing to come clean, to be honest for our *own* peace of mind. What another does with this honesty isn't up to us; we ask God to look after this for us also.

It is time to admit the effect our dishonesty has had on others' lives. It is time to "make up" for the times we have lied, pretended, and tried to hurt or fool those in our lives. It is time to admit our denial of our addictions to control.

We come to make amends. We come to have our amends made with our Higher Power in charge of our honesty.

"Except When To Do So..."

When we were entrenched in our controls we, as controloholics, were very selfish. When we were trying to control, we weren't always considerate of others' feelings or how our actions would affect those around us. We were simply in a tunnel of control, and being in a tunnel, we did not see others clearly; we did not consider others clearly.

Honesty is essential in this Program, but we must remember that honesty is about *us* and *our* actions, not about others and their actions. We do not take on the job of being honest for someone else, we ask for the honesty to come clean in our own lives.

Sometimes, the sharing of our honesty with others will not be appropriate. We, who have been in a tunnel of inconsideration, need to consider whether our honesty is appropriate with each person and situation, where our actions or words need amending. We are not honest in order to hurt — we are honest in order to have our life healed. To push honesty on another is not our purpose. To push honesty where another is not willing or in a position to receive that honesty is not our function. In this step we ask for our Higher Power's appropriateness in each amend we make.

In each case we share what our part has been. We are honest about our part in what needs to be amended. Whatever the other needs to be honest about or to admit, is not our concern.

It may not be appropriate to bring up the past with another person, but it is still necessary for us to make the amend within ourselves. We have come out of our tunnel into the light. Honesty will keep the light shining, but in our honesty we are also honest about our intent to share our amend. Our Higher Power's Honesty will heal, and it is this Honesty we ask for in each amend we need to make.

This is a Self-ish program. It is concerned with a Higher Self or Power guiding our lives.

Admit One

We do not admit our wrongs in order to feel guilty. We admit them, so we may finally see our completeness beyond everything that we have done, or was done to us.

We do not admit wrongs in order to continually feel shame. We admit them so that we do not have to carry that shame any longer.

We do not admit our wrongs in order to *be* wrong. We admit them so we can see that our wrongs are not *who* we are. Who we are goes beyond our wrongs. Our wrongs have been in the way of truly being able to see the Love that we are, the innocent child that is within all of us.

By admitting our wrongs, we finally get to see that we are okay; that there is hope for us; that there is nothing inherently *wrong* with us; that we truly do deserve to be loved, accepted, and included once again.

By admitting our wrongs, we go beyond our *doings* to find our *being*.

We do not admit our wrongs in order to be humiliated; we admit our wrongs in order to find the humility of forgiveness.

We do not admit our wrongs so we can finally be right. We admit our wrongs so we may finally see our strength, our wholeness, and our completeness.

We admit our wrongs, so they may be gently corrected by One who only sees our Innocence.

How Do I Use Thee... Let Me Count The Ways

In a life run on self-will, we have liked to see how people could be of use to us. We have liked to see how they may be used to our advantage. We have liked to see how people could fit in with our plans, and if they didn't — well, then they were of no use to us. We have thought it was up to us to figure out if someone was useful to us or how they may be useful to us. We have thought using people would assist us in getting our own way.

We have used people to fulfill our goals. We have used relationships to fulfill our romantic dreams or sometimes simply as a convenience. We have used our children to fulfill our dreams of success, or sometimes we have forgotten about our children, because they did not fit in with our immediate plan — they were of no use to our current goal.

In business we have used people to make contacts with others. At times, we have used people as stepping stones or as vehicles to get where we wanted to go. We have ignored those who were not going in our direction — they simply were not useful.

We have used friends to do us favors, to lend us money, to solve our problems, to bail us out of difficulties. We have used friends to complain about the state of the world, to listen to our resentments, our illnesses, and our general discontent.

We have used others to make us feel worthy, to make us feel loved and accepted, to make us feel that we belonged and were special. And if they did not fulfill *our* use, then we became angry with them and in some cases abandoned them.

Whatever our addiction, we used others to obtain and support it. If our addiction was drinking, we used those in our lives to further this goal. We have lied, cheated and manipulated in order to use those in our lives to the best advantage, in order to maintain the addiction. And if some people proved to be of no use to us, we simply dropped them for they were no longer useful in maintaining the lies and deception — they became a burden and made us feel guilty.

If we were trying to control in any situation, we would only want those whom we were able to control, those whom we saw as furthering our goal. The rest we had no time for. They were simply in the way — our way.

Even those people that we decided we could use, we did not treat well, for our goal of control came first. If we were using someone to bring us security, then we would take advantage of what we thought they had to offer us. Should they not provide our security, we would become angry, resentful and blaming. And should they not fulfill their use to us, we would feel justified in searching elsewhere for someone else we could use.

We used people to get what we wanted and having used them, we discarded them entirely or kept them until they were of use again.

Understand, we will only wish to use someone if we are trying to control our lives. What *we* use for our goal of control becomes abused. *An abusive relationship is when we try to use the relationship to further our sense of control.*

What is given to God to use as He would have it used, becomes healed.

The addiction of control has led us to many strange uses for our relationships. How do we use those in our lives? It is time to count the ways and to ask that our uses for the relationships be forgiven and released. It is time to let our Higher Power show us the real use for those in our lives. When *we* use someone in our life to *our* advantage, we will not see the gift that person is. When we have no use for someone in our life, we have again lost sight of the gift that that person is. What *we* would use soon loses its use for us, but what we give to our Higher Power for His Use becomes an incredible gift.

We look at how we have been using those in our lives to control things our way. Then we ask that our Higher Power show us the real gift, the real use of that person.

Dear God,

Please take all I have used my brother for,
And replace it with his true value for me.
Please show me the value of his love,
Of his being,
Beyond the uses I have had for him.

Please forgive me my uses,
So I may see both my brothers'
And my own innocence.

Please use Your Healing here,
Where I have sought to control.
Please use Your Care here,
Where I have sought to manipulate.

Please use Your Acceptance here,
Where I have sought to judge.
Please use Your Use here,
Where I have sought to take advantage of.

Amen

There Is One Who Has All The Power

Amends come through you.

Amends come from one source and one source only. This Source is God.

If you are wondering how to admit to a brother, you may ask to make amends thusly:

"God, please heal this situation in Your time and in Your way. Make of me a willing instrument that You may guide to let all amends, all forgiveness, and all innocence flow through."

Then, in all humbleness and all acceptance, give thanks that God's Power to heal is certain and give thanks it will be taken care of in the most appropriate way possible. Then continue to give thanks, fully admitting you do not know how this amend will occur, but you know it will occur.

Take no credit for any amends but give thanks to the One from Whom all amends come.

A prayer of amends is simply this: *"I do not know how my amends will take place, but I know if I turn it over entirely to You, it will take place. I know if I am willing, You will show me my part in this amend precisely."*

Your knowledge of how the amends are to take place is not necessary. Indeed your whole part in the amends is to give them to your Higher Power, and then with thanks, to consider they will be made in the most appropriate way and at the most appropriate time.

The micro course in making amends is:

"I can't. He can. Let Him."

Question: *How do I make someone willing to receive my amends?*

Answer: *You ask for amends to occur and give the time and the place, the means, and the wherefore, to your Higher Power. He will take care of it.*

When you are praying for an amend to occur, you are truly asking that your Higher Power take over completely. You are admitting your willingness to let go of your attempts to heal — to let amends occur through you or simply beyond you. This is the channel you open with asking. This is the willingness that opens for amends to occur.

In other words, you may ask for an amend with someone and at the same time not have to decide how the amend is to occur, only to be willing to open to let it occur.

The key to making amends is asking, giving over, and gratitude. The best conductors of amends are Faith and Gratitude.

Be thankful for all things, for only in Gratitude can understanding and awareness come. Only in humbleness and Gratitude can God's Voice be truly heard.

Step Ten

"We continued to take personal inventory and when we were wrong, promptly admitted it."

When all else fails try admittance...
but before all else fails... try admittance.

Step Ten

The best way to keep a house clean is to clean it on a daily basis. We had not cleaned our "home" for a long time. We had not looked at our attitudes, our controls, our uses, and so some major cleaning had to be done. The accumulation of years of guilt and pain needed to be cleansed. We needed to put our own home in order first.

Now, we no longer wish the accumulation of years. Step Ten is our maintenance step — a moment-to-moment, day-to-day maintenance step. We continue to take our personal inventory and when we are wrong, we *promptly* admit it.

No one likes to be wrong. In fact, we are taught *not* to be wrong; we are taught to *avoid* being wrong. But here in this program, we are encouraged to admit immediately when we have acted with impatience, with anger, with judgment, with control. We are not asked to *be* wrong; we are only asked to admit when our actions come from our old addiction of wanting to control. Another way of seeing this step might be to say: "And when we were trying to be right, promptly admitted it." For wasn't it always trying to be right *our* way that put us in the "wrong"? Wasn't it always wanting to be right our way that caused us to "wrong" so many people?

So we admit we have been wrong about *our* way. Self-will has been "wrong" for us.

Now, each time we are wanting to control *our* way, each time that we react in an unloving way to another, each time we use our anger, criticism, blame, denial and so on, we promptly admit that we have been wrong. These ways have never worked before, and they will not serve us now. We become willing to do this promptly, because we no longer wish to carry the burden of guilt that our controls have brought us. We wish our home maintained on a daily basis. We wish to be able to live with ourselves — we wish to be comfortable in our home.

This step is a maintenance step for *us*. It does not say to take an inventory on others. This is a personal inventory, and with this step we keep our own home in order. In our home there is finally a sense of sanity and peace. We can live with ourselves and what we do. We can finally like our home and be at peace.

And When We Were Wrong...

You don't like to be wrong. In fact, all of your defenses are to cover the times when you have chosen "wrongly". You don't like to be wrong, and you most certainly don't like anyone else to see you are wrong. You would much rather be right. It feels much better to be right. If you could avoid being wrong, you would. But as you are bound to make a few mistakes, a cover-up becomes needed. When you are wrong, it becomes a habit not to admit it. If at all possible, so there is no doubt in anyone's mind, you deny anything that you do "wrong" most strenuously.

When you are hiding being wrong, you will need a lot of explanations and justifications. You become expert at this. You become fluent in being "right". Your defenses are marvelous creations. God forbid that you be wrong, but God forbid even more that someone may *find out* that you are wrong.

You have been taught that it is wrong to be wrong. You have been taught to avoid being wrong, and you have been taught that you would be punished if your wrongs were discovered.

Being right is held in high esteem, but you have seen that being wrong can bring disapproval, and sometimes abandonment. Admitting when you have chosen incorrectly is the same to you as *being* totally wrong. To admit your wrongs seems to imply that your *being* is wrong. The statement: "There is something wrong with him," is a fearful statement to hear, for you have proof that being wrong only leads to disaster and sometimes even death.

It doesn't do to be on the wrong side or with the wrong person. It isn't safe to say the wrong thing or to do the wrong thing. You don't want to wear the wrong thing or give the wrong thing. You certainly don't want to make any mistakes, for isn't a mistake doing the wrong thing? So, you have decided it definitely isn't safe to be wrong, nor admit to anyone else where you have been wrong.

No one seems to be rewarded in this society for being wrong. The rules are: "Don't get caught, but if you happen to be caught — deny like hell. And just in case you are caught, have your story ready with all its justifications, excuses, and make it sound convincing, otherwise you'll be in the wrong."

With these beliefs and proofs it is difficult to see how admitting your wrongs can be helpful. It feels downright dangerous. But we say: Admitting your wrongs is simply bringing to the open all your beliefs and misperceptions that have kept you imprisoned. It is making room for love, trust, joy, closeness in your life. It is, then, an admittance of what is in the way to you having Peace of Mind. It is admitting what has brought you pain and kept you closed. It is finally seeing that it is okay to make mistakes, because what you have made can be turned over to your Higher Power for Him to unmake.

The biggest wrong you commit is thinking you can do it alone without God's assistance. This is truly the only error you have made, but once made, this error is reflected everywhere in your life. Any time you have acted from your desire to have things your way, the outcome will be in error, for it will not be from Peace. Any time you have responded lovelessly to those around you, it is because you have made an error or been wrong in your perceptions.

It is to bring these wrongs or errors to God's Light, so He may dissolve them and guide you in what is appropriate. The only real fear that you have is to be caught with all the things that you have done wrong.

We ask you instead to say:

"Here is where I have been wrong,
Would You please correct this.
My wrongs, my misperceptions can only
be corrected,
If I admit them and bring them to You.

Please help me to admit my wrongs,
So You may show me,
That the only thing wrong,
Is when I choose not to be with You."

Amen

Admission

A few years ago, we were told that admittance was the key. Then we were asked by our sponsor to make a sign in large print: "When all else fails try admittance, but before all else fails, try admittance." We have had this sign on our wall for many years now and the deep significance of this statement only begins to dawn on us.

We have seen admittance as sharing where we are coming from, as confession, as coming clean, as letting the other in, as letting in or allowing Trust and Support to enter. The words "admittance" and "admission" have so much meaning for us now that we start to see why admittance may be the key to recovery. When I'm in a controlling state of mind, using the old symptoms of avoidance, guilt, blame and denial, admittance appears very threatening. Yet to admit One Who has All Power into our lives is the healing. Admittance is letting God in.

— Maynard

"I admit at this time that anytime I feel a tension; anytime there is a commotion around me; anytime I need to blame someone or fix someone, that at these times the separation is because I have chosen to do it my way.

I admit that most of the time I have tried to be in control. I have tried to be in control, because I have wanted things my way. I have tried to convince myself and others that my controls are there, because I did not want to be controlled by their controls. I now admit my controls are there, because I want things my way.

I admit that I create and am responsible for each and every problem *I* see in my relationships. Through my wanting things my way, I have created that which is separate from God. I am responsible for turning over everything that "offends" me in a relationship; that "attacks" me; that "hurts" me; that "forces" me; that "compromises" me; that "fixes" me; and that separates me, so that my Higher Power may show me another way.

I may call this proving, personal laws, useless pieces of information, qualifications, form, whatever — I admit I have created it. With this admission, I now clearly see that blame is impossible. When I have created this, how can it be anyone else's responsibility? When I have created this, how can I blame myself when I have merely chosen incorrectly? All I need do is to choose once again to be with God and His Will. To be free, I now claim responsibility for all I see and for the way I see it, and pass it on to my Higher Power for His Healing. I have created it, and what I see has nothing to do with anyone else. I choose to no longer point out; for the time I spend pointing out keeps me from my own admittance, my own program, and from releasing my illusions.

When there is disharmony between us, I choose to look within to admit I have created this, and to see that I can be willing to see things differently. I am in conflict, when I want control of the situation to have my way. I now see clearly that controlling *anything,* to have my way, will only bring separation, disharmony, distrust, and total lack of freedom. When I come to this realization, I may at that moment choose that, "Thy Will be done," and regain my freedom once more.

If I see someone as trying to fix me, hurt me, ignore me, force me, step on me, confine me... then I admit and see clearly at this time that this, also, I have created and am responsible for turning over for reinterpretation to my Higher Power. And by claiming this responsibility, and asking for my Higher Power's help, I need hide no longer. This is truly where honesty and openness rests."

When we say to take responsibility for your creations, we are not saying to take blame for them, we are only saying — look at them so you may ask for their release.

God is the One to share our feelings of guilt with, for He will take them and remove them.

Continuing To Come Clean

If you are defending anything, you are not coming from Truth.

If you are justifying anything, then you have not fully admitted — you have not come clean.

If you are pushing, you are not coming from center or Truth.

If you close off, you are still into justification, justifying why you are closed.

If you are closed, there is an area you are hiding from Truth.

If you are defending, there is still something you hold — admit it.

If you are resentful, then you would still use resentment to justify why you are not coming from Truth.

If you would hold a grudge, realize you hold it because you have not allowed all the Truth to enter.

If you are sad, you have not told or seen the Truth.

The Truth is not an admittance of guilt, or self-blame, it is any admittance of an area you have tried to manage yourself, an area you have put ahead of Peace.

All resentments are held to justify why you are not telling or seeing the Truth.

It is to come clean for *you*. It is to let go of the resentments to see where you have not been entirely honest.

Honesty is essential in coming clean.

Coming clean means — free from guilt. This occurs when we admit where and how we have sought to control, rather than see Peace.

With honesty comes forgiveness, for it is not to make ourselves feel bad that we come clean; it is to free ourselves from resentment and fear — it is to see our Innocence.

Dear God:

I have not come clean in this area, please bring Your Honesty and Love to wash it clean. I wish to hide it no longer.

Amen

A Controloholic Checklist

If we are trying to control, we will have to "use". The use of any of the following, is a sure sign that we are trying to control a situation.

Trying to control has to use guilt.

Trying to control has to use blame of another.

Trying to control has to use anger.

Trying to control has to use righteous indignation.

Trying to control has to use hurt.

Trying to control has to use being above all this.

Trying to control has to use getting even.

Trying to control has to use demands.

Trying to control has to use withdrawal.

Trying to control has to use leaving.

Trying to control has to use closing off.

Trying to control has to use sarcasm.

Trying to control has to use put-downs.

Trying to control has to use punishment.

Trying to control has to use fear.

Trying to control has to use pushing.

Trying to control has to use avoidance.

Trying to control has to use protection.

Trying to control has to use correction.

Trying to control has to use more control.

Trying to control has to "use".

When we come from trying to control, we will not be able to trust anything.

There is nothing to accomplish except to choose Peace today — and in that state — is All accomplished.

Doing a book that goes beyond controloholism has been very hard on Maynard's and my controls — we just can't get away with using them anymore. Anytime we try to control doing any aspect of the book, we become stuck immediately using all our old controls to get our way.

We've tried to control what went into the book, what should stay in the book, and what should be removed from the book. We've tried to control what needed to be corrected, what needed to be explained and what needed to be illustrated. And each time we tried to control — we used. We used everything on the controloholic checklist and added a few more for good measure.

It's total insanity — with our controlling, neither of us makes any sense, the book doesn't make sense, and the Program doesn't make sense.

But the moment we admit that perhaps we were trying to control, and we are back to using our controloholic solutions, sanity returns. We ask our Higher Power to manage what needs to happen with the book and once again we can see the gift of each other, the gift of this book, and the gift of the Program.
                                                              — Leanne

Pleased To Meet You

We have asked for Life and in our asking we find that anything
that is not Life comes to our awareness to be healed. When we
see and feel these things, we do not have to blame ourselves
or feel guilty or feel that *we* are wrong. In finally admitting
and looking at these blocks, all we are doing is making more
room — more room for Life, more room for Joy, more room for
our True Being.

When the insanities of our old conclusions and beliefs arise
to be looked at, consider: "This is on its way out; it need not
block the happiness in my life any longer."

We do not beat ourselves up with the actions and conclusions
we have used. We do not beat ourselves up with the controls
we find. We do not beat ourselves up for being wrong. Our
conclusions and our beliefs have sometimes been wrong
— but our *Being* is never wrong. Who we are is *never* wrong.
Some of our actions and words have been wrong — they have
been wrong because they have closed off others; they have
closed off Life; and they have closed off God.

Our controls have been wrong for us, because they have left
no room for the All Encompassing Power of Love. Who we
are is *never* wrong. The Life, the Love, the Beauty that is the
center of all of us is never wrong.

When we finally look beyond all those things that have kept
Life from us, we need never be ashamed of our true reality.

What we have done has brought us humiliation. Things we
have said or thought or believed about ourselves and others

have brought us shame. But in looking at these things, in admitting them, and in asking for their release, we will go beyond wrong, we will go beyond shame, and with true humility we will see the person we have always wanted to be. We will finally meet ourselves without shame, without condemnation and without fear.

Once we see past the surface of all our controls and manipulations, we will find the room to *be*. We will meet a person we can love and accept. We will meet someone who has released their shame, their wrongs; and we will find, in their stead, someone who wishes to live in all honesty and in all love. We will meet that real part of ourselves that wishes to learn and discover all that Life has to offer. We will meet the true essence of ourselves.

We are not wrong, but we need to turn over all that has been wrong in our lives — all our beliefs in pain, our resentments, our closed and hurtful attitudes, our beliefs, our conclusions, our controls. We make room for the person we had pretended to be and in the release of our controls, we find we do not have to pretend any longer — we are that person. We make room for the honesty that will let us be. We make room for the realness that will let us live.

Beyond controls, beyond manipulations, beyond our "wrongs", we will meet ourselves. We will meet the Higher Power and Knowing within us — and the encounter will be a Holy One.

Step Eleven

"We sought through prayer and meditation to improve our conscious contact with God, as we understood Him, praying only for the knowledge of His will for us and the power to carry that out."

Ask and all answers will be given.
Ask and you will be shown.
Ask and consider it taken care of.
Have you asked today?

Step Eleven

We have sought many things in our lives. It has seemed that our whole life has been one big search. We have searched for happiness *our* way, and what we have found has only disappointed us.

We have sought excitement. We have sought pleasure. We have sought for relationships that would satisfy us. We have sought for careers that would fulfill us. We have sought for love, and we have sought to be "enough." We have sought to be "right" — we have sought our way. And when all these have failed, we have sought to ease our pain.

In this step, we begin an entirely different search. This is the search, not for *our* will, but for *God's* Will for us. Even in this search, we are not required to find the way to God; we need only ask for God to find us.

We have had many priorities, and we have sought to have our priorities come first. We have sought to prove that our priorities, our way, was more important than anyone else's. We came first, our way came first. Our search is different now. There is really only one priority. The priority is asking for God's Will for us. The search through prayer and meditation is a reminder for *us,* for God has never left us. In our desperate search for what we thought would make us happy, we forgot the most important search — we forgot to *look* for God, we forgot to *be* with God.

We seek through prayer and meditation to improve our conscious contact with God for, very often, we have not been on speaking terms with our Higher Power. We are rusty at speaking to God, at praying to God; and we are rusty at listening to God, at meditating in His Presence. The search is for us. It is towards God and His Will for us, rather than towards our own empty visions.

Our search has been unconscious and our search has been empty, for our search has been away from God. Now we consciously talk to God and ask for His help and guidance in everything we do. We lay aside our priorities and ask only for this. We begin to listen, we begin to open, not to our will but to what God's Will might be for us. We do not ask God to help us to gain *our* way. We pray rather for the knowledge of *His* Way.

The fulfillment we have been unable to find in all our other goals is to be found in this step. The happiness, the love, the connection we seek is here. Our search begins and ends with our Higher Power. We are alone no longer.

We need no strength to carry out God's Will for us — this too is given to us. We are relying on God's Strength now. We are relying on God's Knowledge, and we are relying on God's Will for us — now.

Open Your Day

When you say: "Give us this day," it does not mean: "Give us this day *my* way," it is: "Give us this day *Thy* Way."

When you seek to protect your day, nothing else can come to bless you. All you are left with is protection. If you seek to protect your day, to guard it from interference, God's Guidance will not come to your awareness.

Each morning say to your Higher Power: "Here is my day — please give me Yours."

Open your day to the service of your Higher Power.

Plans

You ask us: "Isn't there some planning we *should* be doing?" We say, the question is not whether to plan or not to plan, the question is: Are you choosing your Higher Power first?

If you plan but do not choose God, then your plans will bear no fruition of Peace. If you decide not to plan and do not choose God, again there will be difficulties. Understand, it is not the planning or not planning that is the question, it is: "Does my Higher Power (Peace) come first into my life?"

Your first thought must be of your Higher Power. If it is of *your* plans or of your plans not to plan, then there will be conflict, for you have chosen separately from your Source.

Yes, definitely plans are needed, for truly there is One Great Plan your Creator has for you, but these plans will only be effective with your Higher Power's guidance. This One Great Plan is what you leave to Him in choosing Him first above all *your* plans.

On Praying To God

Your question was: "How do I pray to God? How do I ask? How do I connect?"

It is time to take Step One in connection with praying to God — you admit you don't know how to pray, and then you are in a position to begin.

Praying to God is to make ourselves aware of His continual Presence.

The first step to prayer, then, is to "Be still and know that I Am God." When you first come to Twelve Step Meetings, what are you told? You are told to, "Listen and keep coming back." This, we say, is very appropriate in praying. Be still and wait for the Presence of God. This you will know by the Peace you will feel. There is no need for words at this time, for you are opening to allow God to become a part of you. Can you see that in this state making decisions by yourself is impossible? You may ask questions but understand, all questions really can be summed to: "God, are you there? I have doubts at this time."

That is why we say: "Be still and know that I Am God." You bring to your prayers only your willingness to listen, and you open your prayers with Gratitude to Him that has created you. All else becomes insignificant before this. You have been asking God with doubts and expectations, and with these doubts and expectations in the way, you have not been able to hear Him.

That is why we say: "Be still and know that I Am God."

Do you want an answer to your questions or do you wish to be with God, where all questions are answered?

You ask for certainty. We say: Be still and listen.

You ask for direction. We say: Wait for the Presence of God.

You ask: "How shall I know? How will these doubts be removed?" We say: With willingness and gratitude — "Be still and know that I Am God."

Being still and knowing that, "I Am God," is resting in Peace in everything you do.

Can you see the dynamic Power and Healing in being at the center of the Peace of God?

What If I Ask And He Doesn't Answer?

*Excerpted from Askceptance © 1988 Maynard and
Leanne Dalderis Published by Vitagenics Institute
Foundation*

*I really had problems with the idea of asking God
for anything. I'd hated my image of Him for so long
that I didn't think he'd even talk to me until I'd been
sufficiently punished for all my sins. It was like
being caught by the police with a glove compartment
full of old traffic violations – now I was really going
to get it. I had done so many things that I was
ashamed of that I thought all these things had to
be atoned for before He would consider speaking to
me. Consequently, I avoided praying to God or even
trying to get His attention. I had said and thought
some pretty nasty things about Him. I was afraid He
wouldn't answer or if He did it would be an answer of
rejection and punishment. Sensing my deep despair
and longing, my sponsor gave me this little poem.
He said that God was always speaking to me even
if I wasn't speaking to Him. My sponsor said that if I
could let go of my fears long enough to ask and truly
hear what God was saying to me, God would sound
something like this...*

— Leanne

My Child:

When you are angry, I will answer you.

When you are filled with fear and resentment, I will answer you.

I will answer you beyond all your fears and misperceptions you have about Me.

I will answer you when you are closed and don't wish your illusions disturbed.

When you have judged yourself as "bad," I will answer you.

When you have judged yourself as "undeserving," I will answer you.

Even when you make mistakes, I will answer you.

I will answer you, not because you are finally deserving, but because you are my child in whom I am *always* pleased.

I will answer you because you are loved.

I will answer you simply because you have asked.

And My answer will always be: "You have done no wrong — my child can do no wrong. Accept My Love for you, for that is what you are."

I will answer you beyond your fears that I will not answer.

If you are angry at Me, it does not matter — I will answer with Love.

If you are afraid of Me, I will answer with Love.

If you are filled with hate and despair, I will answer with Love.

Simply ask to come Home and I will be there to lead you.

If you are lost, I will be there to guide you.

You are so afraid I will not answer because you are angry, fearful, resentful, and undeserving — but that is when I wish you to ask for Me, most of all.

I will always answer you because you are My child and because you are loved.

Ask for Me to come past all your anger, all your confusion, and all your doubts about Me, and I will be there.

Ask Me to come beyond all your fears that I will not come, and I am there.

I am there because I am with you always; and in asking, you will see this.

My child, I will never leave you for you are loved and One with Me.

Feel Free To Feel Free

Higher Power:

Help me to feel a connection with my brother today.

Help me to feel gratitude for all that I have today.

Help me to feel Your Healing today.

Help me to feel the warmth of Your Presence today.

Help me to feel the Joy that is bubbling within me today.

Help me to feel a kinship with all things today.

Help me to feel the answer to all my fears today.

Help me to feel the forgiveness I offer to others today.

Help me to feel total acceptance today.

Amen

So you wish to finally feel free to feel — begin with gratitude and your fears will matter not.

I thought that to stuff and subdue my feelings was the solution rather than the cause of my problems. I just did not know how to feel. Feelings exposed my vulnerability and that seemed to be too fearful. My sponsor asked me to amend the "Serenity Prayer" for a while to:

*God, grant me the serenity to accept and **feel** the things I cannot change...*

— Maynard

Have You Asked?

Question: *If I'm not controlling, how do I make sure everything gets done?*

Answer: *You have forgotten the Power of Asking. We ask our Higher Power to accomplish that which we cannot. We ask for our Higher Power's assistance in accomplishing whatever needs doing today. We ask for accomplishment beyond our controls, for our controls accomplish nothing.*

How do we go beyond our controls? — We ask. How is anything accomplished? — By asking.

We have forgotten the power of our Higher Power. We have forgotten the power of prayer. We have forgotten the power of letting go. We have forgotten to ask.

Question: *I have asked and sometimes it does not get answered the way I want it to. How can I ask so I get the answer I want?*

Answer: *You'll not always get an answer **your** way. In fact, your way is not the answer at all. The answer comes in God's way and in God's time, because only God's way will heal our lives. Be assured that with asking you will always be answered. Be assured that with asking, whatever is needed to be accomplished will be* *done in ways far beyond what we, with our controls, try to manage. We will be answered and the answers will always be gifts to bring us closer to who we are and to the love that our Higher Power is.*

A Sign Of The Times

A few years ago, an opportunity came up for us to invest in an oil well. This, we thought, was a sign from God. We had asked for God to look after us and obviously this was how it was going to happen. God was "telling" us to put our money in this project. Well, we put our money into the venture and the oil well came up dry — we lost our money and our hoped-for riches. We were stunned — wasn't this God's Will for us? Why give us a sign if this wasn't what we were supposed to do?

It took a lot of honesty for us to finally admit that our whole intent in investing was out of greed, out of wanting to control God's support. In our desire to control, we decided that this oil well was what God wanted for us, because this was what we had wanted for us. In other words, we took charge of interpreting God's Will and took control of how God's support should come. We were disappointed, because our way of support didn't turn out. We were trying to tell God how He should support us, instead of being open to His support — His way.

Many people come to us asking about this or that sign — somewhat wiser, we share the following:
— Leanne

So you are looking for direction. You have asked your Higher Power for guidance on a particular outcome and you wait for direction. You wait for a sign: "God, please give me a sign of

Your Will. Please show me something that would indicate that I am doing Your Will."

You like receiving signs. You like looking around you and receiving some sign or indication that you are on the right path. You want to do God's Will. And so, you begin to ask and to look for signs that will point in this direction.

Before deciding upon any major decision, you ask: "Give me some sort of sign that will tell me which direction to take." And when you believe you have "received" the appropriate sign, you are relieved and take it as an indication of the direction you are to go — you take it as a sign of God's Will.

You continually ask for signs. You are on the lookout for the signposts that God will surely give you. You have become very good at interpreting signs. You now believe you know what is a "good" sign and what is a "bad" sign.

You like reading signs, and have become very discriminating as to how they reveal God's Will for you. Obviously, from all the signs, God wishes you to go in *this* direction and not in *that* direction. And if the signs aren't forthcoming, you wait patiently until they will be given, until you can look around you and say: "Ah, this must be a sign I am to do this. This is God's sign to me."

Let us speak for a moment on God's Will. God's Will for you is simply this — He wills that you be in perfect Peace with Him at all times, whatever you happen to be saying, doing, or thinking. If you are doing or open to receiving God's Will, very simply you will know It by this — you will be at Peace, you will feel Love, and you will feel at Home, WHATEVER IS HAPPENING.

The only sign necessary to see that you are doing God's Will is — "Am I at Peace?" If you are not, then you have a goal that is not of Peace and, thus, you do not see God's Will for you. God wills that you be happy, that you be joyful. God wills that there be Ease, because all is done with Him.

Do you not understand? — it is not *what* you do — it is with *Whom* you do it. All your signs are the ego saying: "I would do this or that, because it is God's Will." You look for signs without, when you are not choosing Peace within. Choose Peace and anything you do will be God's Will, because it will be done in Peace and it will be done with Him.

Choose Peace before all other signs, because being at Peace is the sign that you are with God.

Prayer:

Forgive us our signs so we may be with You.
Please give me Your sign of perfect Peace,
So I may go and do everything in Peace,
Knowing you will guide me,
Knowing Your Peace will light the way.
I need no other sign than this.
Please give me Your Peace each moment.

Amen

If you are in charge of interpreting signs — you are in judgment.

If you feel the Peace and connectedness — that is the sign. "Until I see the appropriate signs, I cannot be at Peace."

Looking for signs limits your Higher Power, for the condition is: "I must have a sign before I can be at Peace with God's Will."

It is because your Higher Power can use anything for healing that your signs are unnecessary.

Question: *Does this mean that we cannot ask for anything?*

Answer: *Ask for anything. It simply means that your judgment of whether your prayers are being answered through the use of signs is not needed.*

God Grant Me...

"God grant me the SERENITY to accept the things I cannot change; COURAGE to change the things I can; and WISDOM to know the difference." — Serenity Prayer

God grants us Serenity.
God grants us Courage and
God grants us Wisdom.

We find that we cannot change anything or anyone. But in the changing of *our* mind; we will find everything around us changes. We cannot change anyone, but we find when our attitudes and focus is changed by our Higher Power, then the people in our lives "miraculously" change also. We find we cannot change certain circumstances, but with the changing of our mind, events around us get resolved. We find that when we change within, what has appeared to be outside and unchangeable finds resolution. We find that by ourselves nothing gets changed. But with our Higher Power, our entire life is turned around.

God grants us the Courage and the assistance to change our mind. We have a choice. We can focus on forgiveness, or we can focus on resentment. We can focus on gratitude, or we can focus on what we do not have. We can focus on love, or we can focus on fear. We can be right, or we can ask for another way. We can hold on to, or we can let go of. God grants us the Courage to choose His Will.

God grants us Wisdom to see the difference between what we would try to fix or manage and what His healing can bring. He grants us the Wisdom to recognize Peace, Sanity, Joy and

Release. He grants us the Wisdom to see that it is not the outside that needs changing — it is what is inside that needs changing — our attitudes, our beliefs, our resentments, our perceptions. Our focus has been on dis-ease and destruction, and now we are given the Wisdom to choose Life. We are granted Serenity to see that others cannot be changed by us, but with the help of our Higher Power, our relationships, circumstances, events, and our very lives are healed.

We are granted a new vision. A vision of Serenity, Courage, and Wisdom. We accept that the only change is within us. And with this Wisdom, we will see the world around us healed with our Higher Power's vision.

In gratitude we receive and

in gratitude we extend

all that we have been given.

Step Twelve

"Having had a spiritual awakening as a result of these steps, we became willing to carry this message to controloholics, and to practice these principles in all our affairs."

This is a journey of joining. We join with our Higher Power and we join with each other. Never are we on this journey alone.

Step Twelve

We must never forget that this Program is for *us*. All of these steps are for *us* to follow. We have tried to change the outside world for so long that we have forgotten that it is our mind, our life, that needs changing.

This Program is a program that looks at self and then turns that self over to the Higher Power. It is a program that relies on Self with a capital "S".

We continue to practice these principles for our own sanity. And because we would keep what we have been given, we too must give. The more we give of ourselves, of our story, the more we find we will be able to keep what we have been given.

We can only share what works for us. We cannot tell someone else how to live, but we can share how our controloholism has devastated our lives, and we can share the healing that comes when we are willing to turn our lives over to our Higher Power. We are not here to fix — we are here to share. We are not here to convert — we give, because this giving reminds us of our true choice and our true Solution.

Those moments, when we have truly given up our management, have indeed been a spiritual awakening. We awaken to the strength of God. We awaken to His care and another way of being. We awaken to solutions, to answers. We awaken to another way. We awaken to healing and forgiveness. We awaken to respect and gratitude. And with this respect and gratitude, we awaken to others, we awaken to service.

We have been asleep in our own self-will and management. We have been asleep with dreams of anger and resentment. We have been asleep in selfishness and despair. But with our awakening, we awaken to those who, like us, try to control. We awaken to share another way. We awaken to give what we have been given. And the greatest gift we can give, is the willingness to live by these simple principles that we have been given. Our gift to others is to be ourselves. Our gift is a willingness to go beyond our controls, and our gift is the willingness to share whatever our Higher Power would have us share.

Having had a spiritual awakening — we give. But we do not manage the giving. Here, too, our Higher Power will direct us and give what is needed to be given. This is the Gift of a Higher Power and it is this gift we are now ready to share.

Limit — One Per Customer

Your purpose is to carry the message of Peace. Your purpose is not to judge whether or not someone has "got" the message and to condemn him if he has not.

If you are trying to manage someone getting the message, you will be willing to walk a mile with your brother, but if he has not "got" the message by then — forget it! You might even grudgingly consent to walk two miles with your brother, but then he better get it for sure this time. If he does not, your journey with him is over, and he is classified as hopeless. You look for greener pastures, where the walking is not quite so strenuous.

There is a limit to *your* forgiveness, *your* patience, and *your* love. There is no limit to your Higher Power's patience, your Higher Power's love. You, in your management, give people one chance and one chance only. With your Higher Power, there will be no limit to healing.

We say to you: Walk the entire journey with your brother. Your walk is not to make sure your brother gets the message; your walk is to accept Peace for yourself and extend it.

May The Force Leave You

You still have much to learn in having respect for others.

If someone is not willing to hear you, you cannot force him to listen. This is very simple but you do not respect it. If someone does not listen, you take this as a sign that you are to push even harder.

Without willingness, healing cannot occur and to force anything is to obscure the healing that is there.

The greatest respect you can give someone is to wait in loving openness for his willingness. Extend your invitation and that is all. Your Higher Power will make sure of the most appropriate time for that invitation to be used. You are there for your Higher Power to make use of. It is not for you to decide how the healing should occur.

Yes, many people need healing, but until there is willingness, they cannot hear you. It is not your function to force that healing to occur. It is only to extend in your heart, an open invitation for healing to occur — not the healing you have prescribed — but the healing your Higher Power would see accomplished. In this are you healed, even if the other is not willing. For extending an invitation to someone without the condition that he hear, is a sign of your forgiveness of him.

To wait in patience for your Higher Power to make use of you may seem difficult, but it is this willingness that permits healing to occur and sets you free from your own judgments.

You cannot force willingness. If someone were to come to the Program, could healing occur if he were not willing? If someone were to come for assistance, could healing occur if he were not willing?

Have you not seen that healing occurs when you give up your very definite ideas on how that healing should occur and what it should look like? Have you not seen in the Program, where you did not know how that person was to be healed, but he was healed? Have you not seen in a meeting, where you have not known how the healing was to take place, but it took place? Have you not waited patiently, in both cases, when there was no willingness, knowing that your Higher Power would guide that person to the most appropriate healing for him?

It is not your concern whether someone hears you or not. That is the Higher Power's concern. Your *only* responsibility is the willingness to ask that healing occur, and again in this willingness is *your* healing.

Give another the respect of respecting his willingness. Give the Higher Power the respect of trusting in His ability to bring healing to the other. You cannot force willingness. Willingness to let someone choose willingness is necessary for healing to occur.

> **"My brother — I respect your willingness.**
>
> **My brother — I respect your unwillingness to listen to me. I know you, too, are guided by your Higher Power, and you will hear when you are guided to hear.**

**My brother — I extend an invitation, which
you do not have to accept.**

I give you the respect of choice.

**My brother — I extend my willingness
to let you choose willingness, when the
time is right.**

**My brother — I extend my willingness to
you, so I may be healed.**

**The rest I know is taken care of by the
Higher Power."**

Amen

Extending an invitation to heal is forgiveness.

Patience is not waiting until *your* will be done; it is
knowing your Higher Power will bring about the healing of
all relationships.

Patience is considering it taken care of.

Patience is impossible without this willingness.

Assisting

Excerpted from DO YOU HAVE A MOMENT? © 1988 Maynard and Leanne Dalderis Published by Vitagenics Institute Foundation

> *For me, the following has been the most useful and practical advice for my twelfth step calls. This advice has carried me through many concerns, especially when dealing with those really close to me.*
>
> *I find that "letting go and letting God" does not mean that we are sloughing it off on God, while we stagnate. It is calling on all the aspects of our Higher Power to bring us results in lieu of our constricting management. Viewing God as Peace, Love, Joy, Life, Ease, and especially Enthusiasm, it becomes apparent that letting go and doing it with God is the most dynamic state. The very word "enthusiasm" when we break it up, means "en" or within and "theos" or God — from God within. When we step aside and let the Enthusiasm within us motivate and activate us, much gets accomplished and healing occurs.*
>
> *—Maynard*

You can't help anyone.
God can.
You by yourself can't.
You don't help — God does.
All you do is to allow God to help people through you.
On helping your friend:
You can't help her.

God can.

You may point this out to her.

To help your friend — step aside and let God do it.

Ask and you will be given the words to say.

Ask and what is for the best will happen.

You can't help your friend.

God can.

Let Him.

1. Ask to be of service.

2. Ask how to be of service.

3. Wait for instructions.

ON BEING OF SERVICE

I can't.

He can.

Let Him.

Where is the room for guilt in this?

All you can do is share your willingness to open. Openness comes from God. This brings us back to "How to be of Service: I can't, He can, Let Him".

In being of service use "askceptance" — ask and accept the form your service will take.

That form will always have its basis in Love.

Miracles are of Love. Miracles are of God. Miracles are service in action. True service is God in action.

You are only confused in trying to be of service if *you* are trying to be of service.

Healing is service and service is extending God's Love. If you are feeling responsible for helping someone, you are of no service. Get out of the way.

Guilt occurs when *you* take responsibility for service. Service is not of you, it is through you. To be of service, be willing to be open. Accept Peace and Joy as yours.

To be of service try admittance.

When you are in service, there is the certainty of God working through you. Certainty is obtained by admitting that you do not know but He does.

Why avoid people when you admit you cannot help them?

If you are to help them, say: "God's Will be done."

TO BE OF SERVICE, BE OF LOVE.

Concern yourself not with whether you are being of service, but whether you are at Peace and willing for God's Will to come.

Your service looks outward at that which is separate. Service is Peace within.

If you are at Peace, you are of service.

Your service has been in a physical sense — if you can't see it, you do not believe it. You want proof of your service. You do not realize service is being with God.

To be of service *you* think is to be worthy. NO. Worthiness does not come from service. You are already worthy. Service is extending this worthiness and this worthiness is given by God... and this brings us back to service:

I can't.

He can.

Let Him.

Start from the realization that you are Worthy and be of service with God.

You are trying to figure out how God's Will should be done. Service is not a burden. If you are doing it "right," *you* are not doing anything — God is.

Are you ready to be willing to give up being of service? Let God do it.

You say: "I have to be of service to deserve support." Again we say — what does this have to with service? You have support and service on opposite sides. This is a strange arrangement. Service and Support are one and the same thing. Why do you separate them? Put it this way: To give and to receive are one. To give service and to receive support are One.

Where is the difficulty?

You have been trying to be of service to reach God. We say: Be with God and be of Service.

"Seek ye first the kingdom of Heaven"... and Service, Support, Love, Joy... "will be added unto you."

You don't have to be of "service," you have to be of God.

The certainty comes from God doing it, and the relief that you don't have to.

The Addiction To Treatment

People often come to us looking for a fix. They wish us to fix whatever they think is wrong with them. In most cases, they do not wish a fix in order to change anything. They wish a fix in order to make their present circumstances bearable. Just like a drug addict, who wishes a fix in order to cope with life, some people wish a similar fix in order simply to survive.

As helpers we sometimes get caught up in giving a "fix" to a junkie. It is only a temporary measure, because fixing or using a fix never really changes anything. It simply becomes more addictive. More and more things seem to need fixing and more and more counselors are sought to give the person his fix.

As helpers, we are really here to help those who come to us get in touch with all their inner resources that can provide solutions to whatever difficulty the person has. We are here to direct them to those inner resources, to that inner Completeness, which provides all the answers, once we are all willing to be in touch with it. It may be called God; it may be called a Higher Power; and for those who have difficulties with these terms; it may be called the Higher Self, or the Whole Self. These terms sound intangible, but the truth is — they work. Our fixing does not.

What we try to fix, becomes the addiction or the fix. What we ask the Inner Knowing to solve in terms of healing, brings solutions.

We can only offer this direction of a Higher Power or the Higher Self, to those who come to us, when we ourselves consider the vast reservoir of strength it provides. We, ourselves, need to admit that our fixing does not work but our opening to that place within ourselves where all answers lie, that part which is complete, is the only thing that will provide a permanent change or solution to whatever difficulty we or others are faced with.

If our focus is on fixing, then all our treatments simply become one fix after another, where we become just as addicted to the treatment as do those who come to us. If our focus is on that Higher Self, that Inner Completeness, then appropriate sharing can occur.

If we, or those who come to us, truly saw our completeness or the Power of the Higher Self, then no fixing would be necessary. But as most of us have not too often been in touch with that strength or that completeness, we need to become aware of all that we use, all that we would try to fix in order to go beyond this addiction. It is because we do not focus on completeness or wholeness, on those inner resources, that we, at times, have become addicted to treatment.

It is not to throw out treatment, for even treatment can be used for healing, if we turn it over to that Higher Self in both ourselves and in others.

We become more willing and confident that the Higher Self *is* the treatment and will surely guide us in whatever treatment or sharing is appropriate. We become more aware of that Inner Knowing that is in each of us, and our direction becomes a mutual opening to that Guidance, to that Power that includes all of us.

What we use, without being in touch with that Inner Knowing, with the Higher Self, tends to be abused — it becomes addictive. The form or the treatment becomes more important than the content or the Healing.

Our treatments do not come first. Our willingness to have that Higher Healing occur, is the whole point of two controloholics coming together.

For healing to take place, we finally become reliant on that Higher Self within us to provide the appropriate treatment; and we become reliant on that Inner Knowing within each person to begin to express whatever solutions or answers he or she needs for their own healing. We begin to trust the process — the process of allowing the Higher Self to bring us in touch with the Completeness that is the solution.

The answers are within us. The Completeness we focus on then becomes the treatment for us and for those who ask guidance of us. It becomes a mutual sharing of what works for us, what is the appropriate solution, rather than what needs to be fixed.

Practicing These Principles...

You come to us heavy with guilt. You know the Program
to be the way out, yet even knowing this, you are not able
to help those around you. There is still illness that you see
and healing seems so far away. You yourself feel sick and
disheartened — how can you ever help those you love, if
you cannot even demonstrate the simple principles of the
Program? You feel that you have let the Program down and
you feel you have let the loved ones down.

We wish you, at this time, to examine your goal. Your goal is
to heal yourself through the principles of the Program in order
to heal those around you. With this goal, you have forgotten
that your goal is the Peace of God. You think: "If only I were to
think the right thoughts, I would be healed, and those around
me would be healed also." Even though this goal is chosen
with the best of intentions, we say it is a goal of separation.
It is a goal of separation, because you have taken the
responsibility for healing onto yourself. You have decided what
healing should take place, when it should take place, and how
it should take place, in order to prove you are on the Program.

Let us remind you — you are not responsible for keeping
yourself on the Program. You are not responsible for healing
— your Higher Power is. Your Higher Power keeps you on
the Program, and your Higher Power is responsible for any
healing. You are not.

The guilt and sickness you feel is because you have taken
responsibility for living the Program, implementing the
Program, upholding the Program, and using the Program to
heal others. No wonder your burden is heavy.

It is only up to you to ask your Higher Power to heal each and every situation as He sees fit. The outcome that should occur is given to Him also. You have been demanding a certain outcome in order to keep yourself on course. The outcome is not yours, neither is your direction.

Understand, it is only for you to ask: "I don't know what to ask, but I feel sick and disheartened. Please help me to give all my outcomes to You so that Your outcome be done. Please take all my doubts and remind me when I am the one keeping myself on course that You determine the Course."

You are not asked to do anything alone. You need do nothing but ask, and even in this you will have assistance.

Judge not your progress by the appearance of that around you, but in the midst of all appearances ask to see Peace beyond all that *you* would have happen. Give up your good intentions for Peace. Give up your outcomes and give up your course. Give up your asking and come with an empty cup, asking that it be filled with God's Love and God's Healing.

Poncho Villa Rides Again

Sometimes our sponsor uses light sarcasm and humor to penetrate our noble self-centeredness. This was one of those times when I was convinced that God needed my help and dedication to help Him "save" others. It was a relief for me to see that I was not responsible to help God, but only for a willingness to ask and accept His help for me. My wanting to step on a soapbox and preach to others is still a lingering shortcoming of mine.

— Maynard

Poncho Villa rides again to save suffering souls everywhere. The invasion is set, the crusaders are ready and the ignorant sinners are waiting. Let the crusade begin: the joint has been cased, and the pilgrims are singing: "Onward Christian soldiers, marching as to war..."

So, how are God's little helpers today? Having a nice ride? The cross you are bearing is slipping just a little.

When we said it was time to begin, our intention was not to have you call in the marines. There was no need for you to march into the battle; to confound the enemy. So you are about to set out for truth, justice and the American way — I lend you a phone booth.

Look at yourselves! Did you ever see such a commotion? We ask you one simple question: Are you ready to begin God's work? We give you one simple little hint: God does not need your help. If God does not need your help, why are you trying to force it or avoid it? We give you one simple little answer: Accept the Program, accept God's Peace for yourself.

Simple instructions, but so hard to follow. Never mind. You may keep your horse. The next time you wish to stage an invasion, simply remember: God does not need your help, only your willingness to accept healing for yourself and share this acceptance.

Carrying The Message

We find the following list invaluable to us when we are having difficulty relating to certain people and situations. It's been called different titles — "Seminar Checklist," "Client-Counselor Checklist," "Parent-Child Checklist..." It really doesn't matter what the situation or relationship, we've found that this list has us focus on the true essence of people coming together. I keep forgetting that it's not my pretense that others want; it's my honest sharing and my willingness to let my Higher Power guide me that is the real connection in any encounter. This list never ceases to open my eyes to the true direction, the true healing and the true gift of those who are brought into my life.

— Leanne

Are you with others to teach, or are you there to share?

Are you with others to impress, or are you there to come from where you are?

Are you with others to get, or are you there to give?

Are you with others to preach, or are you there to receive from them?

Are you with others to fix, or are you there to accept?

Are you with others to direct, or are you there to share the moment?

Are you with others to show, or are you there to share love?

Are you with others to show how *you* do it, or are you there to let *God* show you how to do it?

Are you with others to know better, or are you there to learn?

Are you with others to manage, or are you there to let go?

Are you with others to perform, or are you there to experience?

Are you with others to take credit for, or are you there to give gratitude to?

Are you with others to play a role, or are you there to play?

Are you with others to act, or are you there to be?

Are you with others to control, or are you there to see completeness?

Are you with others to share Healing together?

Gratitude

For the gifts we are about to receive... may we truly be grateful.

By The Grace Of God

By the Grace of God, I am given Peace today.

By the Grace of God, I am given Serenity today.

It is by the Grace of God that I may begin, what is needed to be begun today.

By the Grace of God, there is Willingness today.

By the Grace of God, I am given Sanity today.

It is by the Grace of God that I am of Use today.

By the Grace of God I have the Strength, for Forgiveness today.

And by the Grace of God, I can see my Choice today.

I need do nothing to deserve these gifts, for by the Grace of God, they are all given freely — today.

Gracious Living

*Sometimes it's hard for me to find something to be
grateful for. At those times, I have to ask for my
Higher Power's help in showing me some tiny thing
in my life that I can be grateful about. But when my
focus shifts to gratitude, rather than my problems,
I find more and more things I can be grateful for.
Gratitude is such a wonderful opener — it opens me
to appreciating and receiving all the precious gifts
that just keep being given.*

— Leanne

We have to work very hard to obscure the gifts that God
has given us. But we are capable of this. The simple act of
desiring things our way is enough to block *everything*. It is
not enough to destroy it, but wanting to be right can make
us forget our gifts.

What we often forget, is that it is by the Grace of God that all
things are possible. By the Grace of God, Serenity is possible,
Healing is possible, Sanity is possible, and another way of
seeing is possible.

Often we say grace, but we forget that it is by the Grace of God
that all things that are loving occur.

We think we have to earn these gifts, struggle for these gifts,
find these gifts. We even think we are responsible for making
these gifts ourselves. We have many conditions before we
believe we can accept these gifts, for we forget that these gifts
are not of our doing, they are: "By the Grace of God."

God's Grace is really the Gift. It is His Love for us kept eternally — ours the moment we choose to ask for it.

By the Grace of God, we are free. By the Grace of God, all gifts are given to us.

We think it is up to us to begin, but in realizing beginning is by the Grace of God, are all beginnings possible.

We think it is up to us to find Peace, to keep Peace and to maintain Peace. But, when we finally realize, it is a gift given by the Grace of God, we can then be open to accept it.

By the Grace of God, we are sober today. When we try to manage this, we become hopeless alcoholics.

By the Grace of God, there is Sanity today. When we try to find this sanity or keep our sanity, we become hopelessly insane.

By the Grace of God, we are of Use or Service today. When we try to be useful, we become of little use.

It is not what we *do* but what we are willing to receive — by the Grace of God.

> A couple of years into the A.A. Twelve Step Program, I thought myself to be an expert. I could tell everyone how the Program worked and how to stay sober. I was ready to share my expertise. I was what they call a know-it-all. I still wonder how I stayed off alcohol for about seven years. Then came seven "wet" years. My expertise failed me, and I was emotionally bankrupt again.

It was one of those Christmas gratitude A.A. meetings when the sign above the door, "But for the Grace of God..." seized my attention through my hangover and fog. The sign had been there for at least 14 years. For the first time, the significance of the meaning struck a very deep chord. With gratitude I realized that sobriety, serenity and peace were a freely given gift of God. That very moment, the gift of sobriety was mine again. What amazes me to this day is that all my withdrawal symptoms from alcohol were instantly removed. I am grateful for gratitude.

— Maynard

For What We Are About To Receive

You wonder how to let God in — gratitude will connect you. You wonder how to open — an attitude of gratitude will open your heart. You wonder how to ask — we say: With gratitude.

It is impossible to be resentful and grateful at the same time. It is impossible to be closed and grateful at the same time.

When we are grateful, we are open to receive answers to the questions we have asked. When we are grateful, it is easy for all gifts to be given to us. When we are grateful, those around us will wish to give to us. When we are grateful, we automatically give.

It is in the attitude of gratitude, where all giving and receiving take place. Only in the attitude of gratitude, will we see the value of what we have been given.

It is impossible to be trying to get and be open to be given to. These are mutually exclusive. When we are trying to get, we forget to be grateful. When we are grateful, we are open to receive. When we are resentful, we are blinded by our anger.

When we are grateful, our vision is much improved, for we will see the true value of what is in our lives.

We make a new inventory each day. We make a list of all that we have to be grateful for in our lives. This inventory is priceless.

When we are grateful, we are in a position to learn. When we are grateful, we are in a position to go beyond our fears.

Gratitude attracts gratitude.
With gratitude, there is certainty.
Gratitude is the opening,
is the asking,
is the answer,
and is our prayer.

Gratitude is being with God.

How do I pray? — with gratitude.

How do I ask? — with gratitude.

How do I live? — with gratitude.

How do I let go? — with gratitude.

How do I hear God's direction? — with gratitude.

How do I find happiness? — with gratitude.

How do I find healing? — with gratitude.

To walk with God — walk in gratitude.

For Your Consideration

On the road to recovery we are asked to consider another way. We are not asked to know another way, or to make ourselves choose another way, or even to take responsibility for another way. We are only asked to consider that there may be another way beyond our controloholic addictions.

Consideration opens us to solutions — we don't have to accept these solutions, but in our consideration of them, what is true and appropriate will guide us.

In the next section, we share certain ideas that have been helpful in our recovery. We invite you to consider them.

Jackpot

While travelling in Nevada a few years ago, Maynard and I stopped in a town called "Jackpot" to do a "little" gambling. We had it all figured out. We would only play the nickel machines, we would have a limit of ten dollars, and we would confine our gambling to a few hours — that way we wouldn't get caught up in the gambling fever. We knew about gambling addictions, but with these restrictions we didn't think we'd have any problem controlling our impulses. All went okay for the first while, until we got hooked — on winning, on the adrenaline rush, on the sound of sirens, and on the sound of all those lovely quarters hitting metal. As soon as we won, we did not walk away with our winnings, but gambled it all away, trying to get that beautiful sound of a jackpot again.

At 3:00 a.m. in the morning, we had passed our "few" hours, and had graduated to the dollar machines. We reasoned we were not really hooked, because we had only lost $50.00 each, and we weren't much over our limit. But then we both recognized that old feeling of desperation that we knew so well from our drinking days. Yes, so far we hadn't lost much but that old addictive feeling with all its denial and rationalizations was there. We had thought we wanted to win and couldn't understand why after winning, we didn't just walk away. Recognizing an addictive behavior, we asked our sponsor what was happening, and were given the following piece of advice on gambling...

— Leanne

You are convinced you are in the casino to win money. At times, you do indeed win money, but immediately lose it again. Something does not quite make sense to you, yet you feel drawn to gamble more and more. You become desperate and obsessed with obtaining something. You think it is money, but we say let us look at what you are after a little more closely.

First of all, we wish you to admit your addiction to gambling, and we wish you to see you cannot manage it. It gets progressively worse. Your fear and desperation is directly proportional to your attempts to manage your addiction.

You are confused, because you believe you are here to win, but yet continuously lose. We say — you are not here to win, you are here to lose or sacrifice your money in exchange for power, for control.

Look at it this way: Is it for money that you gamble, or is it for the power you think it brings you? As soon as you win money do you walk away, or do you continue until this money is gone? We say: the addiction is the search for power, for control. When you "win" it gives you a feeling of great power and control. It is the magic of being in control against all odds. It is a heady feeling, but it does not last long, for soon you lose and with that loss goes your power. You become even more desperate to find it again. The money becomes the sacrifice you gladly lose in order to find that power again, in order to feel in control again. *What you are really doing is exchanging abundance for control.* You become willing to sacrifice any amount of money just to have that feeling of control once again. This is the addiction.

It is the same with all addictions. With the addiction of eating, you are not eating for nutritional value, you are eating to gain a feeling of control over what seems to be happening to you. You sacrifice health or well-being in order to have control over some area of your life. With the addiction of drinking, you do not drink yourself into oblivion because you like the taste; you drink because it seems to bring you some measure of control over events in your life.

Understand, the addiction is to controlling.

In an addictive relationship, "love" is sacrificed in order to control the relationship. Obtaining control becomes much more important than a healthy relationship.

Let us simplify everything. Any attempt to control will be followed by an addiction. That is why we say: You are not here to win, you are here to control, and you will sacrifice anything to obtain that control. Control demands sacrifice, and the more you wish to control, the bigger the sacrifice required.

Understand this — when you seek to control, you cannot let in Abundance, for you have sacrificed it. You cannot let in Health, you cannot let in Serenity, you cannot let in Well-being, you cannot let in Love, you cannot be Who you really are; for you have sacrificed all these things in order to have control.

At this point, we ask you to see the reverse is true. With the willingness to give up having to control, and this will be the control of anything, you'll be able to let in Abundance, Health, Serenity, and Love. Their sacrifice will no longer be needed.

When you say: "I am willing to do anything to win," you are really saying: "I am willing to sacrifice anything to gain control or power."

When you say: "I'm willing to do anything to make this relationship work," you are really saying: "I am willing to sacrifice anything in order to control this relationship."

We wish you to see that you have been asking for exactly the opposite in your desperation for control. Your addiction is to control or manage your life. It is here you think your safety lies. What we are trying to show you is that any attempt to control merely asks for your sacrifice of all you would truly wish. Try to control anything, and you lose the very thing you are trying to gain by your control. Only your Higher Power can give these things, and they can only be given if you are willing to give up your control of your difficulty. Your safety lies in being willing to see control brings you nothing but desperation; a desperation you soon become quickly addicted to.

IF YOU ARE HERE TO CONTROL, YOU ARE HERE TO LOSE. It cannot be any other way.

Let go of your control of winning and let Abundance in. Let go of your control of alcohol and let Serenity be with you. Let go of your control of any relationship and let Love enter. Let go of control, and you will have indeed hit the Jackpot.

Are You Positive?

We have found ourselves dreading each day, dreading the future, and resentful of the past. We have found ourselves cynical and distrustful. We have found ourselves fearing the worst and feeling hopeless about any improvement. We have found ourselves feeling and expressing every kind of negative emotion.

We have also found ourselves trying to be positive, trying to look on the bright side. We have found ourselves struggling to keep a positive outlook. We have found ourselves trying to smile — trying to grin and bear it. We have found ourselves trying to overcome our negativity. We have found ourselves resisting our negative ways and trying desperately to make everything right.

And, we have found that ultimately, neither our negativity nor our positive affirmations worked. We simply replaced one master for another. We simply replaced one control for another. We have excluded negativity and thought that was the answer. We have tried to manage our negative thoughts and found them more prolific than ever. We have tried to manage being positive, and while at first we felt the difference, we found more and more energy went into keeping our thoughts positively oriented.

Whether we exchange our negative drinking for a positive career; whether we exchange our negative addictions for a "healthy" exercise program, we still find much effort and much control is required — we find we only exchange one addiction of control for another.

We, in this program, find we must go beyond positive thinking, for positive thinking is still thinking we can manage our lives. We find we must admit that we can no longer control what is negative or positive in our lives — we must ask for help.

We had been trying to affirm that we could do anything if we just put our minds to it. This had appeared to be so, until we noticed the effort and denial involved. In trying to manage staying positive, we found we could not admit to our doubts, to our feelings of fear and insecurity, and in not admitting these things, we kept them with us.

Now, we find we must ask for our Higher Power's help in everything. We admit our negative thoughts and feelings so our Higher Power may remove them. We do not deny these feelings. We do not try to overcome them — we let our Higher Power give us His Love and Forgiveness instead.

We do not maintain our new awareness or focus, we do not manage the changes in our perception. We ask our Higher Power to maintain our new-found Peace and happiness. We ask for our Higher Power to change any thoughts, conclusions, or beliefs that have kept growth and healing from us. We admit everything, both positive and negative for our Higher Power's management.

We find we must go beyond positive and negative, for that is still in the land of judgment.

We do not ask our Higher Power: "What is the right or wrong thing to do here?" We ask: "What is the most loving thing to do here?"

We do not ask: "What is good or bad for me here?" We ask: "What is the most healing thing for me here?"

We do not ask: "Should I stay or go wherever I am?" We ask: "Show me Your release and freedom here."

We do not ask to see only the good in a person, we ask: "May I have Your forgiveness here so I may see the Innocence."

We do not ask: "Show me what feels right here." We ask: Please show me that anything that I give to You can be used for healing. Please show me Your Love here. Please show me the gift in each part of my life."

We do not ask: "Please show me how I can get my way here." We ask: "Please show me Your Will here."

Yes, a change of focus is needed. We need to go beyond that which is negative, but we need also go beyond our positive management, to receive the gifts that our Higher Power would gladly give to us and maintain for us. We need to admit everything into His care, for only when we give both positive and negative into His care can anything in our lives be changed and set free.

Let's Get Willing

Anytime you are into management or trying to control, things become "serious".

Can light come in where things are serious?

Being serious is touchy business. When you are serious, you become "touchy" about the area you are serious in.

To be serious, there is an insistence on having it done "right".

When you are serious, you are not open, you are in a tunnel.

When you are serious about something, you are easily offended. When you are serious, all sorts of things upset you. When you are serious, it is inevitable that you will judge yourself unfairly treated. When you are serious, it is inevitable that you will judge.

When you are serious, you will not see support but will only see having to carry on alone. It is most difficult to forgive — when you are serious.

You think that seriousness and willingness is the same thing, but we will show you the difference. *Willingness* is the opening to have things accomplished. *Seriousness* is closing in order to do it your way.

Seriousness can get very heavy.

You have been taught that getting serious is a prelude to doing anything worthwhile. But we say: Becoming willing is what is truly necessary for anything to be done. It is the difference between doing something with Ease or with tension or dis-ease.

Seriousness checklist

Things may be "serious" if you find yourself:

— upset

— easily distracted

— defensive

— easily thrown off balance

— suspicious

— walking on eggs

— tense

— running out of time

— lacking/not having enough

— feeling alone

— feeling unfairly treated

— closed

— desperate

— short of breath

— overwhelmed

— lost

— having deadlines

— having no time for others

— having no time for fun

— surrounded by darkness

— having a feeling of impending doom

— not understood by others

— not appreciated

— surrounded by people who don't seem to care

— surrounded by people giving you a "bad" time

— having an insistence on doing it "right" / on doing it the "right" way

— being a perfectionist

— being above everything

— angry

— feeling slighted or offended

— pushing or procrastinating

— or any other "serious" endeavor

When you get serious, all of the above apply.

It is not to make light of what you find serious, for you do not make light— God does. You ask for God's light to enter in whatever area seems serious to you. You ask for another way to be given. You ask for assistance in giving up the area that has become serious.

Seriousness is a sure sign that *you* are managing.

Seriousness and enthusiasm are mutually exclusive.

When we say: Lighten up! you do not have to manage this. You would even make this serious.

Peace is not serious business, for serious business has been *your* business. Peace is letting in God's light, the lightness that comes when we give Him our burdens.

Remember, it is called *enlightenment* not *enseriousment*.

Sickness is a result of taking things seriously.

The worst state to be in healthwise is to be in a serious condition. In other words, you take your condition of wanting to be right seriously.

"Doctor, how serious is he?"

We find it interesting that doctors will speak in terms of "conditions." They want to know what our condition is. Unwittingly, they have put their finger on the very problem — our having conditions. Any condition we put on life will bring us dis-ease or create our "condition". We found only one condition that is worse than having a serious condition — having a critical condition.

Acceptance

Let us speak on acceptance.

Acceptance lets everything come through and dissolves that which is not of Love.

Acceptance makes no exceptions, everything is looked at without judgment and accepted as being the way it is supposed to be at that time.

"God grant me the serenity to accept the things *I* cannot change." By myself, I can change nothing except my willingness to change. It is necessary that I accept everything, making no exceptions. I admit, I accept, and I ask God to remove that which is not of Love.

"God grant me the courage to change the things I can," knowing that all I need do is to be willing to ask God for His assistance. The courage I need is to admit where I have been wrong or mistaken.

I am now willing to accept God's acceptance for me.

There is nothing you may not accept. Anytime you say, "This I will not accept," you have placed a limitation or a judgment on yourself or another. Acceptance does not mean being stuck with, acceptance means seeing things as they are *now* without judgment.

It is so important to accept yourself. You have made lists or conditions of those things which are unacceptable to you;

you have a list of what must be fulfilled before you find yourself acceptable.

We say, you have it backwards. Acceptance always comes first, for it will dissolve anything unlike itself. As with admittance, acceptance begins within.

To the extent that you do not accept yourself, you will find others not acceptable. That is why we say — admit and accept that which is within. This is truly turning admittance into acceptance, for with acceptance admittance is no longer necessary.

I Take Exception To Acceptance

Some of you have great difficulty with the thought of
acceptance. Somewhere in your thinking you believe that if
you open up to acceptance, then you will also have to *condone*
whatever is let in.

You have the belief that acceptance of where you are requires
that you be stuck there. You have the belief that whatever idea
you let in, you will have to believe it or accept it as being true.
You have the fear that whatever suggestion or direction is let
in, you will be required to follow it. Acceptance to you means
— game over. To you it means the loss of all options and the
point where you have no other choice, but to be stuck where
you are, and even worse — be required to like it.

You have the belief that to accept someone is to condone all of
his behaviors and actions. If you accept someone, you believe,
then it means to you that you have condoned whatever he
does as being right, as being true.

You resist acceptance of things very much for all of the above
reasons. You think acceptance means being stuck and having
to like it. You think acceptance means an end of choice,
and you think acceptance means having to condone either a
person, idea, or circumstance.

Let us look at what acceptance is all about. Acceptance is a
willingness to let in. You let in, in order to have God or the Life
Force come through. When you let in or accept, this Life Force
can then reinterpret anything that is causing you pain or fear.
What you are really accepting is that there is always another
way beyond what you are feeling or seeing.

Acceptance, then, means — we let in, in order to have another way. We accept where we are in order to go beyond. If we resist where we are, the Life Force cannot come through. We do not accept where we are in order to find happiness in being stuck there. We accept where we are in order to have the Life Force show us another way.

We let in suggestions, again in order to let the Life Force come through. When we accept or open to another's suggestions, then there is no resistance. We can either choose to follow them or let them go. To accept another's suggestions does not mean we have to agree or disagree with them; it only means we are considerate of them. We are not stuck with having to keep them. We let the Life Force come through with our acceptance and whatever suggestions are appropriate for us, we will be open to. Understand, we are never required to keep suggestions, for even the ones we choose to follow are also given over or allowed to flow through. We are "stuck" with nothing.

Many of you greatly resist accepting others. You think: "If I accept someone, then I also have to condone what he does. Even while I may accept most of what he does, there are still some things I do not condone. I would not want him to get the impression that I approved of these things."

The idea of unconditional acceptance is most appalling, while you believe you have to condone another's actions. Understand, acceptance does not make anything right, nor does it make anything wrong. To accept someone simply means that you are willing to see the Truth about him beyond what he does and beyond what you see.

Acceptance may be likened to the flow of a river. If we dam(n) the flow or resist it, there is struggle or pain. But if we let the Life Force through, we are gently guided and shown solutions beyond that which we have been resisting.

Acceptance, then, is letting in the Life Force for the Healing of all our perceptions. It does not take away choice, but it shows our choice. It does not take away Freedom, but it shows Freedom. It does not leave us stuck, but it lets in all solutions. We accept there is another way, and we accept it will be given.

How Is My Spiritual Growth?

We were sitting in a seminar listening to the lecturer describe the seven levels of consciousness that we, on our spiritual journey, must pass through. My sponsor whispered in my ear, "He's forgotten level eight." "What's level eight?" I whispered back. My sponsor smiled and answered, "That's the level where you finally realize there are no levels."

— *Leanne*

Spirituality is unconditional. You cannot be a spiritual being sometimes. You are spiritual when you are feeling highly enlightened. You are spiritual in the depths of depression. You are spiritual in the moment, and you are spiritual in the midst of confusion. The only difference is that, at times, you tend to lose sight of your spirituality.

One person is not more spiritual than another. One may be more in touch with his spirituality, but that does not make him more spiritual — it only makes him more awake.

We all have the same capacity for spirituality — and this is maximal. An enlightened being is one who is in touch with his spirituality. As we all have the same Source, we all have the same Spirit. In this are we all connected.

When we forget to put God first, we lose the knowledge or connection of our Spirit or our Spirituality.

I've Had Enough or I've Been Had By Enough

Wanting very much to make my life work, I enrolled in many workshops and seminars to the point of becoming a seminar junkie. At one of the most "prestigious" seminars, the leader mentioned that in her work and consulting practice she had discovered that at least over 80% of her clients had the belief of not being enough as the root of most of their problems. It varied slightly from "not being enough" to "not being smart enough, rich enough, big enough, successful enough, sexy enough"... and so on. Whatever the specifics, the core was the same of "not being enough".

I identified with that immediately and proceeded with the rest of the class to find an affirmation that would change around that personal negative thought. I spoke and wrote several pages of statements like, "I'm enough. I'm good enough. I now, in this time and place am completely adequate." as well as some fancier statements, all with the result — I still didn't feel enough.

Then I consulted my sponsor and asked him to help me formulate the appropriate affirmation to make me enough. My sponsor just laughed and said that would be quite impossible, because I wasn't enough and no statement could make me become enough. The answer to my dilemma came when my sponsor elaborated. He said: "By yourself you are never

*enough, but with God the question does not even
arise — with God you are complete." Wow, what
a relief!*

— Maynard

One of your strangest beliefs is the belief in enough. You
seek to have enough money, security, friends, excitement,
education, preparation, contacts, success, attention, love,
time, peace, space, food, variety, stimulation, recognition,
acceptance, and so on.

Your society is based on having enough, doing enough,
looking enough, sounding enough, accomplishing enough,
and being enough. One of your biggest desires is to be "good"
enough. More than anything else, you wish to be good enough
at whatever you do. And your greatest fear is: "What if I'm
not good enough?"

In all your search have you ever questioned: What is enough?
If you were to question this, you would soon find that when
you are into the idea of enough — there is *never* enough. If
you are trying to be good enough, have you not noticed that
you never succeed in feeling enough? There is never enough.

What we wish you to see is that enough is based on the fact
that you are coming from lack. If you want to have or be
enough, then obviously you are coming from a place where
you are having neither. Enough always comes from proving,
and what you prove is: "I'm not good enough." As soon as you
think of enough, you think of what you do not have or what
you are not. Can one ever have enough money if you are trying

to have "enough" money? Can one ever have enough love or affection if you are dealing in trying to have "enough"? As soon as you think in terms of enough, you think in terms of not having. As soon as you try to be good enough, you are doomed to failure because you begin by seeing a lack. And when you come from lack, this is what you perceive everywhere. Lack is thus perpetuated.

Sometimes you say: "I've had enough!" But where do you draw the line? Again, how much is enough? Sometimes you ask us: "How much pain is required before I can leave a situation? How much struggle is enough before I can have Peace?" Enough is always seen in terms of sacrifice. You have to sacrifice to be good enough; you have to sacrifice to have enough love; you have to endure pain enough in order to have Peace.

What we truly wish you to see is that the pursuit of enough is an illusion. You will never have enough of anything, for the belief in enough is based on lack and separation. Then we ask you another question: Would you rather have enough, or would you rather have All there is? Would you rather be enough, or would you rather know your true power? When you pursue being enough, you lose sight of What or Who you are.

So, you'll never be good enough, rich enough, happy enough, successful enough, secure enough... but in giving up this pursuit you may begin to see you have a choice for All there is. Please give up your chase of enough. Please give up your resentments of having had enough, and in giving these things up, we are asking you to see the freedom you have in opening up to receiving All there is.

Prayer:

Please take my belief in enough,
And give me Your completeness.
Please take my trying to be good enough,
So I may see my wholeness.
Please take my belief in enough,
So I may see I am your Child,
In Whom You are always pleased.

Help me to see,
I can never do enough,
Be enough,
Or have enough,
Because it is mine already.
Please show me my inheritance,
That goes beyond enough,
To a connection with Oneness.

I am not enough,
Because that is not Who I am.
I am not enough,
Because I am complete in You.
I am not enough,
Because I am given freedom.
I am not enough,
Because my Integrity within is so much more.
I am not enough,
Because it does not matter.
I am not enough,
Because Who I am is based on Perfection,
Is based on Completeness,
And is based on having ALL THERE IS.
I've had enough of enough!

Please show me beyond this belief,
So I may know Who I am.

Amen

When you think of Peace, the idea of *enough* does not even enter at all. When you think of forgiveness, *enough* disappears. When you are thinking by yourself and in charge of your own security, you will think in terms of "enough". When you choose Peace, again, enough is not even considered because you are connected with your Source. It is laughable to say: Do you have enough of your Source? Being with the Source is Everything.

So the question again becomes: Do you want enough, or do you want Everything?

Trying to be enough is impossible — it is like chasing a carrot at the end of a stick. It is like saying: "I will be happy down the road." As long as you start from not having enough, you start from lack. And in starting from lack, how can you ever feel fulfilled? You can only be Who you are — wholly loving and having everything to give and to receive.

In saying you have had enough, you are saying you have had enough pain in order to ask for something different. But what if you could ask, without the need to maintain having what you consider "enough" pain?

Do not ask what is enough here, but ask what is appropriate.

Enough automatically implies lack.

Enough is dependent on the outside. Appropriateness comes from within.

Ask simply to do what you want to do with Peace and Joy, and leave the ego struggle of enough to your Higher Power to dissolve.

The ego will always tell you Peace is not enough, but in choosing Peace, enough does not arise because everything that happens, everything that you do, is appropriate.

One is a hopeless search — the search for enough. The other is a constant connection which will show you the appropriateness of whatever you wish to do, and whatever you choose to do from Peace will be appropriate.

Self-Esteem

Working on Self-esteem is having gratitude. With gratitude for God and all He will manage for us, we will find our Self-esteem.

Self-esteem is also humility. Thy-Self and not my-self be done.

When we give up judging ourselves and begin to accept ourselves wherever we are coming from, we will be in touch with our Self-esteem.

We will not find *our* self-esteem, for that has been made up of guilt and judgment. We will; however, be given our Self-esteem which is the gift of being with God.

Home Free

You can never have freedom *from* anything. You cannot have freedom from fear, for your freedom is still based in fear. You cannot have freedom from want, for intrinsic in this is the belief in want. If you want freedom from something, it is not really freedom that you are after, but rather getting away from what is causing you discomfort. Getting away *from* is not freedom.

Freedom is finally seeing — there is nothing to get away *from*, only that which we give away *to* our Higher Power. Freedom is not getting away from what we fear; it is seeing *beyond* what we fear.

Freedom is not away from the darkness, rather freedom is towards the Light.

If you wish to be free from fear, your focus will be on fear, not freedom. You will continue to create fear to be free from. Freedom has nothing to do with fear. It has everything to do with seeing choice. We finally see that we have the choice for our creations or for God's Creation. Truly, it is by choosing the Peace of God that we see our Freedom.

You want freedom from your beliefs — but we say this will only make your beliefs seem real. Why would you wish freedom from that which is not real? Truly, freedom is seeing beyond our beliefs.

Freedom is a gift and with this gift we are free *to* love, free *to* be happy, free *to* live. We finally see there is nothing to be freed from.

"Dear God:

I wish to be free.
My freedom has been freedom from fear.
But Your Freedom is the Freedom to Live.
My freedom has been running away.
Your Freedom shows,
There are only shadows that I thought
were real.
My freedom has been avoidance.
Your Freedom is where I can bring all
my darkness,
For Your Light to dissolve.
My freedom has brought fear.
Your Freedom will bring only Love.
My freedom has been a prison.
Your Freedom is a gift that sets me free.
Please show me Freedom is to be
with You."

                                          Amen

Freedom Versus Options

Freedom is only freedom when it is "Thy Will Be Done." All else is a form of bondage. You can only have Freedom when you are willing to give up *your* freedom, for *your* freedom is another way of saying: "My will be done."

You have asked for peace and speak of freedom in the same breath. You wish peace, but more than this you wish *your* freedom. We say, truly, you are not speaking of Freedom; you are speaking of options. You wish to choose God's peace and have the option of choosing your way should peace not meet with your standards. In other words, you wish to let go, let God, but want the option of maintaining *your* will. This you call freedom.

You declare angrily to each other, "I want the freedom to do this or that. I want the freedom to do it this way or that way! Give me my freedom!" What you are truly saying is that you want to maintain your option to do things your way, and you do not wish the other to interfere with this way. True Freedom is choosing to let go of all *your* options in order to have the Peace of God. Freedom does not come from the ability to choose to do things your way.

Yes, you have the freedom to choose "Thy Will" or your will; but only choosing "Thy Will" will bring you Peace, will bring you Freedom.

Yes, you have the option to do things your way, but do not confuse this with Freedom. You are truly free only when you give up responsibility to your Higher Power for *your* freedom.

We invite you to give others freedom to choose as they will, not because you wish them to choose their own will, but because you set yourself free in turning another's decision over to your Higher Power.

Milking It

You have one reason and one reason only for keeping your control — you still believe it has a use for you. You still believe you can use it for something, and you wish to "milk" it for all it is worth. As long as you believe there is some value to be had from the control, you will keep it.

The main function of control, in your perception, is to release you from responsibilities that you have chosen to carry. Instead of giving these responsibilities to your Higher Power, you have decided they are *your* responsibilities. And when the responsibilities become too much, you decide to take a break and a disease is created.

Effort and trying to manage go hand in hand with control, for to control anything takes much effort. And to relieve your discomfort of controlling, another discomfort of disease is called upon. Once you find a use for disease, you will have difficulty letting it go, for you never know when you may need it again in order to control.

You keep disease for the control you think it brings you. Genuine feelings are not to be discredited. They are to be looked at for reinterpretation and release. But if you find that feelings of sadness and grief, pain and suffering can be used to control others, you will not wish to let them go.

You will keep feelings of sadness to milk them for all they are worth. You will keep feelings of grief to control others' sympathy and attention, and you will keep feelings of suffering in order to assure others are there for you.

The question truly becomes: Are you willing to give up control of any situation in order to be healed? Are you willing to see all the uses, all the "milk" you thought you could obtain from all these controls — is the disease? Any use you have for a disease, merely maintains it.

Your first step is to honestly admit your use for any disease. Your second step is to ask your Higher Power to show you another way of seeing safety and inclusion to replace what you have made. And the third step is the willingness to let healing take place.

The more you "milk" a situation, the more you will need to keep the disease. The bottom line for any healing is simply this: "Thy Will, not mine be done."

God Does Not Give You The Solutions — God Is The Solution

A solution cannot be given to you, for that is the addiction. Solutions aren't given to you, for God has all solutions. Thinking that we must have the solutions is the greatest addiction of them all.

You say: "Give me a solution so I'll know what to do." But it is really: "You are the solution that will work here."

Help yourself — to God's gifts.

This is a Self-Help Program because we are willing to help ourselves to God's gifts.

"The Lord helps them who help themselves." — to His gifts.

Do You Have A Moment To Be In The Moment?

Any attempt to control is an inability to be in the present.

Any attempt to control is believing that it is impossible to be in the present — to be in the Now.

Any attempt to control is not seeing that there is a choice.

Any attempt to control harbors an unwillingness to forgive — Now.

Any attempt to control is really an addiction to the past and the future. It is impossible to be addicted Now.

Any controloholic will say to you: "My problem is getting a fix now!" We say — no. The problem is anticipating what is going to relieve the problem in the future, based on what has seemed to relieve the problem in the past. However, the controloholic is not living in the Now.

You cannot be addicted Now.

It is only when you are attempting to live in the past or the future that addictions manifest.

It is to let go in the Now.

We can only look and let go of the past — now.

Controloholics are not in the Now.

Being in the Now requires honesty, forgiveness and acceptance — it requires letting go.

Controloholics do not like looking at things Now. Any difficulty is postponed to the future or blamed on the past.

An addiction is an inability to look at where you are at Now.

Now always expands. Past or future always narrows or limits perception.

Any addiction is an avoidance of the Now.

If we come from the Now, then things unfold. If we come from trying to manage the past or future, then we become addicted to the solutions.

It is impossible to be addicted in the Now.

You say: "But right now I'm feeling withdrawal and that's in the now." We say: There is a difference. Are you actually in the Now, or are you thinking now of the past or future? There is no withdrawal coming from the Now.

Where are you coming from right now? — the Now — or thinking about the past or future?

Of course, you can only come from the Now, for that is all there is. But in your avoidance of being in the Now, much pain and addictions occur.

If you come from living in the Now, healing occurs. If you come from thinking about the past or future right now, there is dis-ease.

This moment are you in the moment?

Are you grateful for Now?

Wanting to control only comes from the past or the future. Coming from the Now, there is a release from control.

You think you can control Now. You think you can want to control Now. We say — no. What you are really thinking of this moment is the immediate future. To get control Now, you still have to think of the future to maintain control.

Coming from the Now, control does not even enter the picture — everything simply is.

It is to ask yourself: "From what state of mind do I come? Am I making decisions coming from the Peace of Now, or am I making decisions based on managing the past or future?"

It is not that you sit in one place afraid to move, afraid to make any decisions, but it is to see that in being in touch with the Now, in being centered in the Now, decisions, actions, and events will occur with Ease, unfolding with the flow.

Past and future is an attempt to manage God's creation. Only the loving thoughts are true or real. And these you will remember Now.

An addiction says: "I don't want to look at this now." All addictions keep Now as far away as possible.

Now is another name for God.

Any time you are confused, full of fear, and frustrated, say:

"I'm willing to be here in the Now.

I'm willing to see Peace Now.

I'm willing to let go Now.

I'm willing to be aware of everything Now.

I'm willing to see what this moment holds.

I'm willing to awaken to this moment Now.

I'm willing to let in the entirety of this moment Now."

Do you have a moment to be in the moment?

Our Solution Is The Addiction

**"...Probably no human power could have relieved our..."
controloholism.**

*I remember the day I hit "the bottom" with taking
drugs. I was up to a bottle of valium a day and
probably would have continued, if only the pills
worked. But that day they didn't. The most
frightening thing was not the amount of drugs I was
taking — it was that the pills no longer worked. They
didn't stop my feelings, they didn't numb my fear
anymore. My solution of drugs wasn't working, and
I was terrified. I had reached my "bottom". I could
either die or ask for another way — I asked. I can
see, now, that my desperate solutions lead to death.
Today, I want to choose life — I want to choose the
solution of a Higher Power.*

— Leanne

Our solutions are addictive.

Trying to do it ourselves or without God <u>is</u> the addiction.

Withdrawal occurs when we give up our solutions that we
have been using, but we are not still convinced that they are
not solutions.

Withdrawal is not freedom from addiction.

Any attempt to control is a state of withdrawal. When we try
to control our lives, we begin to withdraw from society. By

the same token, if we try to manage to stop our attempts to control, then we go through the state of withdrawal.

Trying to control is a withdrawal from God's assistance; it is thinking we must manage to do it ourselves, and to do so we withdraw into our own resources.

When we give our desire to control to God, by the grace of God we are again joined with others; and we are again joined with Sanity. We are no longer withdrawn nor do we experience withdrawal.

What is withdrawal if not the removal from God's presence?

Total freedom from addiction occurs when we truly want another way and, by the Grace of God, are given it.

In other words, we finally see our solution is not a solution at all.

The consideration that we cannot manage our lives with our solutions, is the answer to recovery from all our addictions.

Whether we do it on our own by relying on our own resources, or by relying on those around us — understand, it is still a reliance on our solutions rather than God's solution.

THIS IS THE ADDICTION.

Transference from one addiction to another occurs when we are still addicted to *our* solutions. The entire recovery rests not on getting rid of the addiction, but on seeing only God's Solution will work. Getting rid of addictions is still *our* solution.

It is not to get rid of the addiction in order to get on with things. This is the mistake of many addicts. It is; however, to give up things or our solution, which is the addiction, in order to have recovery.

As soon as we decide for *our* solution, we no longer have a choice; we have become addicted.

The moment we think, "I must do this by myself," we will use our many addictions as a solution. To put it bluntly: As soon as we decide to do something with *our* solutions, we are hooked.

It is by the very reason that we are saying, "I must do something," that we become fearful and nothing gets resolved.

The moment we are open to God supporting us and giving us His Solutions, then we will notice how very much is accomplished.

"There must be another way. God show me!", is the release from all addictions.

All gifts that we both give and receive come from God. Because of this, there is an unlimited supply. All of *our* solutions are limited, and the more we become addicted to them, the more limited will they be.

Reaching bottom is the seeming frightening realization that our solutions do not work. The fright comes because we still desperately want them to. The release comes when we ask for another way to be given to us.

Whatever is given — if we make it *our* solution — then we have missed the point and again are addicted to our solution, whether it be work, therapy, religion, or any other solution. However, if we continue to ask for God's Solutions, then there is no addiction.

Our solutions are an addiction to form. God's Solution is to put the Spirit of Love, Trust, Integrity, Joy, Ease... first. In other words — Peace, the Peace of God comes first.

When we think we have to do something by ourselves, we procrastinate or we push as a solution. We use drinking, drugs, anger, work, eating, blame, as a solution. However, if we are open to receiving God's Solution each day, our addictions are released. In order to have a 180 degree turn, we must see our choice at the pivot point. The pivot point is either "Thy Way or my way be done."

"I Am" Here In The Midst Of All Things

In the midst of all things is the Peace of God.

In the midst of your blackest imaginings, your worst feelings of terror, is the Peace of God.

When it is said to choose the Peace of God above all else, there is no separation involved. Truly you see the Peace of God in everything. There is no place where It is not.

You do not have to deny your illusions or feelings, merely be willing to consider the Peace of God is in the midst of them.

You do not have to believe this. It is true without your belief.

Your choice is not Peace on one side and your controls on the other. It is Peace in the midst of your controls; it is Peace beyond your controls.

Your goal has been to protect your fearful feelings from exposure. You thought your armor brought you peace. We say it only brought you an illusion of safety. Peace is everywhere.

Your focus has been on your protection. This you have called peace. We say that your choice truly is to see God's Peace or the Light in everything. It requires simply a change of focus. "When you truly want Peace, you will see only Peace." This is what we mean by focus. *It is not for you to deny or to get rid of your feelings of fear; however, your choice is to ask for God's Peace even here.*

The choice for Peace never pulls you apart, for Peace may be seen everywhere.

Peace demands no sacrifice.

We are not asking you to let go of anything yourself. We are asking you to consider Peace in all situations, to see that letting go to a Higher Power may take place with this choice.

If you are willing, letting go to God occurs with this willingness.

To find your Higher Power, it must be realized there is no place where your Higher Power is not.

We will ask you specifically to be willing to feel the Peace of God, for nothing else will penetrate your controls, your fears at this time. Be willing to feel the Peace of God in all situations.

If you are afraid you will lose Peace, or not feel it, ask your Higher Power to look after it for you. Ask God to look after *your* letting go to Him.

Your choice is simply this: Be willing to consider there is the Peace of God in all feelings, situations, people, fears, frustrations, mistakes, anger, pain, and all other imaginings. Your willingness to have the Peace of God given is the only choice you need make.

Consider It Taken Care Of

Consider letting go of *your* controls.

Consider a Power greater than yourself.

Consider a solution being given.

Consider giving your life and will over to the care of God.

Consider it taken care of.

Conclusion

Nothing's Changed

So, you have sought to control again and nothing has changed. You thought that after due consideration of the twelve steps, something would have changed. You thought that after all your willingness to give up your controls and turn them over to your Higher Power, something would be different. But here you are using the same old solutions and having the same desperate feelings accompanying them. You are back to square one. You are back to using controls and you are discouraged — "Where is the change? Where is the progress?"

Let us gently point out one truth to you — control never changes. Management never changes. The results will always be the same. When we seek to control, all our old "solutions" will be there. When we seek to manage, all our old patterns with all their craziness will be there. The use of controls does not change anything. The moment we choose control rather than the principles of the Program, rather than our Higher Power, we will see immediately that nothing has changed.

But you see, that is the whole point of this Program. Our controls ultimately have never worked nor will they ever work. It is like the alcoholic who decides to drink again. Even after many years following the Twelve Step Program, he will find that after the first drink — nothing has changed. The same feelings, the same addiction is still there.

When we choose *our* solutions, we will find nothing has changed, for *our* solutions don't change anything. We'll find ourselves back to square one, back to Step One, back to finding our lives are out of *our* control.

But, the great gift of this Program is that it does not matter that we have chosen our solutions again. We have seen there is another way that changes everything. We have seen a way beyond what we have tried to change and could not.

No, the results of controlling *our* way do not change. Management does not change. But we may choose the principles of this Program at any time, and in this choice do we go beyond our patterns and our fears. It is the difference between night and day. Darkness does not change, but our desire, our willingness to let in the Light of our Higher Power will make the darkness disappear.

We Admitted Another Human Being

By ourselves, letting go of controls becomes too much for us. We need another human being to keep us on track. We find it is helpful to have a sponsor — someone in the Program who has seen beyond controloholism. This person, too, has led a life built on self-will, but our sponsor, through following the steps, has found another way and is now ready to share the experience and the way that has worked for him or her.

When we find ourselves caught up in a desperation of wanting to control, it is helpful to talk to our sponsor to get another way of seeing the situation. Our sponsor helps us do the steps and points us in the direction of our Higher Power. Sponsors share what works for them, and they share what their lives were like before considering the Program.

We find we need to share. We find we need to admit another human being into our lives. We find we need to let another person see us for who we truly are. We have held too much inside for too long. We have kept our hurts and our fears inside for long enough. We need the guidance of someone who has experienced what we feel now, but who can show us another way beyond our desperation.

We find it necessary for our own sanity and peace of mind to have someone we may call on anytime, when we are into our old ways of self-will and control. We need a sounding board.

We need someone, who like us, is willing for another way and is prepared to let a Higher Power guide his or her life.

We find our sponsor will frequently call us on our use of control. Our sponsor will point out, when we are trying to get our way, rather than asking for our Higher Power's solution. We find that our sponsor will let us get away with nothing. We can no longer use our old controls and our old justifications. This we find is our salvation — we can no longer use our cons, our excuses, and our denial.

We ask our Higher Power to bring an appropriate sponsor into our lives. In this, too, we ask for guidance. We become willing to admit another so that our own admittance may come faster and faster.

We, who have avoided looking at many areas of our lives, will find the love and care that a helping hand can bring in, shining a light on our journey home.

Lifeline

There are many things you hold on to, thinking they are your lifeline. You are convinced that business is your lifeline. You are certain that home and family is your lifeline. You are positive that connections are your lifeline. You take it for granted that having control is your lifeline.

You cling grimly to these lifelines, afraid to let go, afraid you will lose your grip. What you have failed to see is that all these "lifelines" are frayed at the end and are attached to nothing. You keep wondering why you continuously sink into conflict and drown in pain, while you valiantly cling to these lifelines.

It is simple. These things are not your lifelines. Your Lifeline is your Higher Power. Your Lifeline is the Program. The lifeline is not business, homemaking, relationships, connections, controlling. It is not trying to manage. The only Lifeline that will work is the Peace of God — are the principles of the Program.

You ask us: "What is my life's work?" We say: Go to meetings. You say: "Sure, but what is my life's work?" We say: Meetings come first. Go to meetings, choose Peace, and the rest will follow. You say: "But what about my business deals? What do I do here? What about my finances? What about my home life?" We say: Go to meetings. Choosing Peace and following the Program must come first, because they are your lifeline, and without this lifeline, you will continue to drown in your own management, no matter what area you are in.

All these other things are not your lifeline; they are not your goal. Your goal is Peace. Your Lifeline is letting go to a Power that can manage your concerns. Continue to go to the meetings that will point this out to you.

I Need A Meeting

At various times during the day, we sometimes get that feeling of being off balance, of wanting to control, of needing something. At these times we have an expression — we say we need a meeting.

There is something that occurs when we meet with others who wish to go beyond using their controls, and who wish to find solutions to their difficulties. When we find ourselves feeling alone and fearful, we need others to remind us that there is another way. We need a place where it is safe to come from wherever we are and to express our willingness to be given solutions. We need a place where it is safe to share and let go of our past. We need a place to share and be reminded of our Higher Power through others' sharing.

We find we need to meet with others, so we do not forget that the use of our controls does not work. We need to meet with others to find ourselves and to find the Presence of something higher than ourselves. We need to meet to see the way clearly again. We need to share our grievances, so we do not hide them, and so they do not grow within us. We need to share our joys that a life built on gratitude and letting go to our Higher Power can bring.

We need to express ourselves. We need to allow ourselves to be, and we need to find the acceptance for others in their being. We need to share how we have used and tried to control. And we need to share the miracles that are given when we let our Higher Power run our lives. We need to be seen, and we need to see. We need to be heard, and we need to hear. We need to listen. We need to have our hearts touched, and we need to touch the hearts of others.

We cannot find ourselves, and we cannot find God alone. We need the spirit of others. We need the Faith, Trust and Support of others. We need the laughter and tears of others. We need to be and to let be. We need to hear our Higher Power speak through others, and we need to let our Higher Power speak through us. We need to see ourselves in each other.

We need to give, and we need to receive. This cannot be done alone. We need reminding each moment of the gifts that are ours. We need a Power Greater than ourselves, and we need a Spirit that works through everyone. We need to love and be loved.

When we are feeling alone — we need a meeting. When we are in despair — we need a meeting. When we are full of gratitude — we need a meeting. When we are full of fear and hatred — we need a meeting. When we have something to give — we need a meeting. When we are closed and bitter — we need a meeting.

We wish to be healed of a life run on self-will and conflict. We need to share ourselves, and we need the sharing of others for this healing to occur. Our Higher Power has given us many gifts, and to keep them He has given us the greatest gift of all — He has given us the gift of each other. To receive and keep the gifts we will be given — we need a meeting.

*Today I have no doubt that meetings are my
lifeline. After seven years of sobriety, I started
missing meetings — I soon started drinking. To us*

controloholics, with a history of substance abuse, missing meetings can be as fatal as walking in a bog of quicksand.

By the grace of God, I'm clean today. I no longer find it trite when anyone calls out: "Keep coming back!" at the conclusion of our meetings. Knowing that meetings are my lifeline, and this reminder my saving grace, I too say: "Keep coming back!" When I want to avoid meetings, that is when I need one the most. That is when I ask for the willingness to go. I have not regretted having gone to a meeting yet.

Whether a meeting is between a couple of controlohlics over a cup of coffee, or in a more formal setting with a larger group; whether it lasts five minutes, an hour, or more, it does not matter. It is the sincere communion, the sharing of a commonality that is the miracle that heals.

— Maynard

If You Want What We Have Been Given

None of us *has* the Program — it is given to us. None of us ever *"gets"* the Program — it is given to us. Each day is a gift given to us, when we are willing to receive it. When we forget that Serenity is a gift, then we lose sight of it. When we think we have to "have" or "get" the Program, then we are no longer "on" the Program.

None of us ever has it made — it is given to us. Each day we ask for this gift. We don't have to get it, we don't have to make it — it is given. Anytime we think we have the Program, we find ourselves back in control once more, back in trying to manage our lives, back in conflict again.

We do not receive Peace alone. It is given each time we are willing to give — of ourselves, of our time, of our story. It is in sharing our own doubts, our own frailties, our own mistakes, our own misperceptions, our own controls that we become willing to ask for this gift again. We share with others that, although we, too, face the same fears, the same conflicts, the same anxieties daily, there is another way that can be chosen instead.

We show the simplicity of simply asking. We show that amidst our controls we may ask God to relieve us of them. We share our laughter at ourselves and show there is no mistake so big or so awesome that cannot be forgiven or released.

We do not receive the gift of Peace alone. Our daily mistakes, our daily tribulations and struggles can all be used for healing, so that the gift of Peace can be seen once again. No, we do not have it made — we have it given. The same power for destruction is still there. The same fears, the same patterns. But when we ask, we are given another way; and with this asking do our fears and patterns drop away. And what has been destructive becomes a vehicle for our sharing, for our story, and a reminder there is a better way.

"If you want what we have been given and are prepared to go to any lengths to ask for this gift, then you are ready to receive another way."

Beginning Again

We are never finished with the steps. We use them each day. They are our compass to sanity. In each situation we begin with Step One, and in each situation all the other steps follow. Each step is reflected in whatever step we are choosing to focus on. Each step is an integral part of all the other steps.

We are not discouraged that we are not finished with the steps. We are grateful that the steps are there for our journey, always.

We are not finished with the steps for we will begin them again. But we are finished with our lives that have been run on self-will.

This is not an end. It is a beginning of another way — another way that grows clearer each time we are willing to consider the steps once again.

Just For Today

Just for today I would like to see whatever needs to be accomplished — accomplished.

Just for today I would like to do whatever needs to be done — just for today.

Just for today I would like to be open to the Joy and the gifts of the day.

Just for today I would like to be present instead of managing to be somewhere else.

Just for today I would like to give up what I *have* to do in order to see the *Ease* of doing.

Just for today I will ask for the strength to do one thing that needs doing.

Just for today I will ask to be centered for one moment.

Just for today I will take time to be here — just for a moment.

Just for today I will ask for the willingness to do one thing I have been putting off.

Just for today I will give myself the freedom not to *have* to do anything and in this freedom I will be open to whatever is most appropriate to do.

Just for today I will recognize Who does the doing, and
— just for today I will be grateful for whatever it is that has
been done.

Just for today let me see I need not manage the doing.

Just for today let me give up my desperation of what needs to
be done in order that Thy Will be done.

Just for today let me feel that what You do is what is most
important in my day.

Just for today let me give up my day so I may receive
Your day.

Just for today let me see that what needs doing most of all is
giving all my management to You.

Where Do We Go From Here?

*Having compiled, read, re-read, and shared this
book with some of our friends, Leanne and I are just
starting to realize how much we need this Program
ourselves. We also realize that just occasional
reading of this material is not enough to nurture our
new-found budding life "beyond controloholism". We
recognize a need to give this Program away to keep it.
To fill this need we started a weekly meeting, using
this text. We meet at our home, welcoming others
wishing to go beyond their controloholism.*

*We also attend other Twelve Step group meetings
such as: A.A. (Alcoholics Anonymous) and Al-Anon,
E.A. (Emotions Anonymous), and N.A. (Narcotics
Anonymous), to name a few. Each day, there are
many other new fellowships starting based on the
Twelve Step Program. We find them all nurturing,
because regardless of the addiction, the twelve steps
really do work, and we find ourselves welcome in
their "open" meetings. We feel we never need to be
alone again since there are Twelve Step meetings in
each city on this continent and these fellowships are
listed in most telephone directories. It gives a great
sense of belonging knowing that our extended family
is only a phone call away.*

*We are deeply grateful to Alcoholics Anonymous for
having pioneered this Twelve Step Recovery Program.
We feel grateful to A.A. for having gone through the
labour pains of group and fellowship growth and for
freely sharing their Twelve Traditions as guidelines*

*for any twelve step group meetings and conduct. We
are grateful that with these tools at our disposal,
no one needs to lead a life of quiet desperation any
longer. With this Program, no one is deprived of the
opportunity to come clean, to choose life, and to find
the Peace of God.*

— Maynard

A Meeting Grace

Dear Higher Power:

Please conduct this meeting for healing.
Should we not know how to conduct this meeting,
Take that ignorance and use it for healing.
Should we *think* we know how to conduct this meeting,
Please take that ignorance, as well, and use it
for healing.

Should there be undue interruptions,
You can use those interruptions for our healing.
Should, seemingly to our senses, nothing happen,
Please take that "nothing" and use it for our healing.
Should we feel compelled to use our controls,
Please take those controls from us and show us
Your Guidance.

We admit we do not know how to work this Program.
Please open our hearts to it every step of the way.

Please take *our* faith and show us *Your* Faith.
Please take *our* trust and give us *Your* Trust.
Please take *our* integrity and make us Integral.
Please take *our* management and give us *Your* Support.
Please take *our* separateness and join it with
***Your* Wholeness.**
Please take *our* fears, so they don't hide *Your* Love.
Please take *our* wanting to please and give us *Your*
Gratitude and Certainty.
Please take *our* controlling nature, so *Your* Peace
may enter.

It is You and not we who corrects our mistakes.
It is You and not we who removes our shortcomings.
It is You and not we who brings healing to
these meetings.
It is You and not we who knows how to be.

And now, please give us Your Willingness to begin this
meeting — Your Way.

Amen

FURTHER SHARING INFORMATION

Watch for the following books by the same authors on Kindle and Amazon in the near future:

Where is Your Worth?

Do You Have a Moment?

Askceptance

Opening to Healing

Letting Go One Step at a Time: Beyond Controloholism

The Gift Book

Guideline Productions Inc.
Calgary, Alberta, Canada
e| dalderis@vitagenics.ca
w| www.livingwithguidance.ca

Maynard and Leanne are open to further sharing of this material through: **seminars**...**workshops**... **group sharings**... They may be contacted at dalderis@vitagenics.ca.

AFTER CONSIDERING THIS BOOK

Letting Go One Step at a Time
Beyond Controloholism

We would like to introduce you to... The Gift Book available on Kindle and Amazon.

If you would like to read more about the gifts that await you "beyond controloholism", you may wish to order this inspiring book describing God's infinite Gifts.

> *The Gift of Ease*
>
> *The Gift of Wonder*
>
> *The Gift of Being in the Moment*
>
> *The Gift of Strength...*

There are 110 Gifts and their descriptions, in this book, for your consideration.

What is "beyond" our controls?

All of God's Gifts — waiting to be opened!!!

www.ingramcontent.com/pod-product-compliance
Lightning Source LLC
Chambersburg PA
CBHW052031090426

42739CB00010B/1866